ORDNANCE SURVEY LEISURE GUIDE

COTSWOLDS

▲ Cottages at Upper Slaughter

Produced jointly by the Publishing Division of
The Automobile Association and the Ordnance Survey

2 AA/OS COTSWOLD GUIDE

Editorial contributors: Ruth Briggs (The Cotswold Countryside); Dr Philip Dixon MA, D.Phil., FSA (The Ancient Cotswolds and Roman Roads, Towns and Villages); Ted Fryer (What are the Cotswolds?, Managing the Landscape and The Cotswold Way); June Lewis (Cotswold Villages, A to Z Gazetteer and Gazetteer revisions for new edition); Mark Richards (Tours and Walks); Rebecca Snelling (Fact File). Short features: Barbara Blatchley; Dr Philip Dixon MA, D.Phil., FSA; Ted Fryer; June Lewis.

Original photography: S & O Matthews and Forbes Stephenson

Phototypeset by Wyvern Typesetting, Bristol
Colour separation by Fotographics Ltd.
Printed and bound by
BPC Paulton Books Ltd.

Maps extracted from the Ordnance Survey's 1:63 360 Tourist Series, 1:25 000 Pathfinder Series and 1:250 000 Routemaster Series with the permission of Her Majesty's Stationery Office. Crown copyright.

Additions to the maps by the Cartographic Department of The Automobile Association and the Ordnance Survey.

Produced by the Publishing Division of The Automobile Association.

Distributed in the United Kingdom by the Ordnance Survey, Southampton, and thePublishing Division of The Automobile Association, Norfolk House, Priestley Road, Basingstoke, Hampshire RG24 9NY.

The contents of this publication are believed correct at the time of printing. Nevertheless, the Publishers cannot accept responsibility for errors or omissions, or for changes in details given.

First edition 1986
Reprinted with amendments 1990
Revised edition 1992
Reprinted 1993, 1994

A CIP catalogue record of this book is available from the British Library.

AA ISBN 0 7495 0382 3 (hardback)
AA ISBN 0 7495 0372 6 (softback)
OS ISBN 0 319 00288 8 (hardback)
OS ISBN 0 319 00279 9 (softback)

Published by The Automobile Association and the Ordnance Survey.

Introduction: Bourton-on-the-Water

Contents

▲ The Promenade, Cheltenham

Introduction

The Cotswolds, with their distinctive village architecture and enchanting landscape, are an enduring microcosm of Britain's past. Reaching back to Roman times and beyond, they have in more recent years become a popular tourist haunt. This book will help to enhance the pleasures of a visit, guiding the visitor through the history, traditions and wildlife of the Cotswolds. It lists and describes their towns and villages, marking out the routes of walks and motor tours which seek out the hidden corners and the finest scenery. Written entirely by people who live and work in the Cotswolds, and backed by the AA's research expertise and the Ordnance Survey's mapping, this guide is as useful to the faithful who return to the Cotswolds year after year as to the first-time visitor.

What are the Cotswolds?

From the Dorset coast to Yorkshire in the north lies a belt of oolitic limestone, laid down in ancient seas. At the widest part, where the land has been tilted up on its western side to form an escarpment with a gentle dip slope to the east, is the area known as the Cotswolds. Although most of it lies in Gloucestershire, five other counties share in this area of 790 square miles.

To today's visitors 'Cotswold' means warm-coloured stone, satisfying architecture, a feeling of peace, comfort and well-being, an upland landscape – but tamed. But former travellers from Shakespeare to William Cobbett and Sydney Smith found the hills wild, bleak and wearisome.

Country living may have been simple but not necessarily idyllic, if we are to believe the following catalogue of tasks from an 11th-century manuscript (mentioned in the Cotswold Countryside Collection at Northleach).

'In May, June and July men must harrow, spread manure, set up hurdles, shear the sheep, make good the fences and buildings, cut wood, clear the ground of weeds, make sheep pens, construct fish weirs and mills. During the next three months they reap, mow, set woad in the dibble, thatch and cover the crops, clean out the folds, prepare the sheep pens and pig sties and ploughs. During the winter they plough, in frosty weather split timber, prepare orchards, put the cattle in stalls and the pigs in sties, set up a drying oven on the threshing floor, and provide a hen roost. Finally in spring they graft, sow beans, set a vineyard, make ditches, hew wood to keep out the wild deer, set madder, sow flax and woad, and plant the vegetable garden.'

It was the Industrial Revolution which created such unpleasant urban conditions that places like the Cotswolds appeared to contain a sanity fast disappearing in the cities. As the 19th century turned into the 20th many people wanted to 'get away from it all'. Community life held its attractions then as now – a mirage of simple country living.

In 1892 Ernest Gimson, who trained as an architect in Leicester and London, and his friends, the architects Sidney and Ernest Barnsley, moved to Sapperton, where they felt that building and the crafts, cabinet-making and blacksmithing for instance, could be combined in a way not possible in the usual urban architectural practice. They produced furniture of splendid design and craftsmanship and also built the village hall. This is an excellent example of keeping to the old style, making it blend with its neighbours almost to the point of being unnoticeable. Some of the original furnishings are inside.

C R Ashbee brought his Guild of Handicrafts – a previous generation of London's East-Enders – to Chipping Campden in 1902. It lasted a few years before it broke up but had a considerable influence. One workshop still survives today, run by a grandson of one of the founding members.

With the decline of the woollen industry in the first half of the 18th century and, later, the growing mechanisation of agriculture, people moved off the land into often more lucrative employment in the cities. Motor-cars have taken over from footpaths as the country dwellers' route to work or to their relatives in the next village. In searching for our rural roots, we can now experience the delights which our country forebears created but were not always able to enjoy. And what are those delights? Here are just a few.

High vistas and river valleys

Views across miles of rolling upland in all directions. Some high points advertise the distances you can see – on a clear day! From Broadway Tower it is said you can see 12 counties (13 before the local government reorganisation in 1974) – southwards across the Thames valley to the Wessex Downs; south-west to the Mendips; west to Wales; north-west to the Malverns and the Clee Hills in Shropshire. On a clear winter day with the sun low in the sky, the light reflects from blocks of flats on the southern edge of Birmingham. A pair of binoculars provides a view of these blocks looking like a futuristic army marching towards the Cotswolds.

Walkers take a break and enjoy the view towards Crickley Hill.

From wide vistas to the more intimate enclosed view. The Isbourne rises on the wilder slopes of Cleeve Common and winds its way northwards through Winchcombe to Shakespeare's Avon.

The Frome cuts its way from south of Witcombe Woods, through the remoter farms and woodlands around Miserden and westwards into the industrialised Golden Valley. On its way to Stroud it passes almost alpine settlements on the steep hillsides.

The watershed between the Thames and the Severn lies along the western scarp, so most rivers run eastwards to the Thames. The Bristol Avon rises, like its Thames-bound sisters, and flows eastwards through the Cotswold villages of Sherston and Easton Grey. It then leaves the hills to follow a clockwise turn through Malmesbury, Chippenham and Melksham before returning at Bradford-on-Avon and the Limpley Stoke valley near Bath.

The Thames tributaries of Evenlode, Windrush, Leach, Coln and Churn will reward the visitor with secluded villages and winding valleys with more open expanses on the plateaux above.

Seven Springs near Cheltenham is the source of the Churn and is, in fact, the remotest source of the Thames. However, the commemorative stone in a field to the north of Kemble and the Foss Way proclaims that spot as the official underground source. The statue, replaced by the stone, has now been removed to St John's Lock near Lechlade.

Tracks

The Cotswolds have a long history of settlement, and it is interesting to discover how our ancestors used to get from place to place.

Prehistoric routes can be traced, such as the one we now call the Jurassic Way from the south-west to the north-east. It links many important places of the day such as the Rollright Stones near Long Compton and the Stone and Iron Age hill-forts of Crickley Hill. Later the Romans imposed their road system, which was so good that much of it lies under our present-day tarmac roads. However, to the east of Tetbury there are parts of the Foss Way which did not comply with the requirements of later times and so reverted to tracks, which make good footpaths for us now.

There are tracks for special uses, such as saltways. Look on the map for Salter's Hill, Saltway Farm, Saltridge. A major route (from which others diverged) from Droitwich to the Thames valley crosses the Cotswolds between Hailes and Lechlade. It is mostly tarmacked and can be travelled by car. Other tracks were used as drove roads for animals, or for medieval 'wool trains' of packhorses carrying wool from the Cotswolds to the Continent.

With the big thrust to improve the roads in the 18th century came the turnpikes. Toll-houses are still a familiar sight with their windows which allow the turnpike keeper to look along the road in each direction. One such house to the north of Bishop's Cleeve still displays the charges. Like motorway developments today, turnpikes were not always appreciated at first. Nash in his account of Worcestershire (1799) relates:

'It is not surprising that when turnpikes were first erected, and tolls taken, that the common people should be disgusted and riotous, but after some few persons had been executed for cutting down turnpikes at Ledbury and Tewkesbury, the farmers and gentry finding the roads gradually mended, the aversion subsided, and all were contented.'

Architecture

The Cotswold vernacular is a type of architecture that has evolved within the Cotswold region over the centuries rather than sprung up in response to fashion. It is difficult to define precisely, but if you think of an accent or a dialect as the speech peculiar to a district, then the vernacular style is the architectural equivalent. It is the architecture of the indigenous craftsman, based on local tradition, suited to the needs and character of the inhabitants, taking into account the climate and social conditions, and using the building materials of the region.

Of the grander buildings that reflect the vernacular, Owlpen, south of Stroud, is a beautiful example of a Cotswold Elizabethan manor-house. Late 17th-century style is evident at Dyrham Park, a National Trust property, and 18th-century classical at Dodington Park.

Owlpen Manor and its church nestle into a hollow of the wooded hillside.

Batsford Park, just north-west of Moreton-in-Marsh, is a good example of a 19th-century Cotswold Tudor mansion, and Rodmarton, built by Ernest Barnsley, is representative of the 20th century. By contrast, Sezincote has an exotic flavour, with its onion dome said to be the inspiration for the Brighton Pavilion.

If simpler buildings take your fancy, Chipping Campden, Marshfield, Northleach and Wotton-under-Edge have outstanding almshouses, which proliferated in the 17th century. The bus shelters at Farmington and Nympsfield are also worth a visit.

The latest buildings are often of artificial stone as the villages expand to become, to some extent, outlying commuter suburbs of many cities.

Churches

There is endless enjoyment in these monuments to social change, let alone religious significance. Walk down the naves of St James at Chipping Campden and St Peter and St Paul at Northleach and you may well conclude that they were designed by the same person. The stained glass at Fairford is a marvel. Gargoyles in wood and stone, such as the imp on the choir screen at Winchcombe, illustrates the humour of the sculptors as well as their skill. Misericords under choir seats in some churches show scenes of medieval life.

The brasses at Fairford, Northleach and Campden tell stories about the notable locals, such as wool merchants. Brass-rubbing is an enjoyable pastime, but always ask permission first. Some churches augment their income by charging a fee, while others prohibit rubbing because of wear and tear. Substitute copies at brass-rubbing centres still produce excellent examples to remind you of your visit.

Festivals and customs

Cotswold towns and villages have many celebrations, fetes, flower festivals and open days during the year. Here are some with more ancient backgrounds.

Dover's Hill, above Chipping Campden, is the scene for Dover's Games, a modern-day revival of Robert Dover's Cotswold Olympicks dating from James I's time. Apart from the fun of the event, including shin-kicking, the torchlight procession is unforgettable.
Cooper's Hill, near Brockworth, has a slope of

Cheese-rolling contest at Cooper's Hill.

one-in-one. What better place to chase Double Gloucester cheeses from the maypole at the top to the St John Ambulance waiting at the bottom! This is a hair-raising entertainment for Spring Bank Holiday Monday.
Cranham has a feast and a deer roast in August.

At Bisley on Ascension Day the wells are dressed with garlands of flowers.

Bisley has seven wells issuing from a decorative stone well-head set in a bank. On Ascension Day the wells are dressed. Although this was inspired by the Derbyshire custom 100 years ago, do not expect to see pictures made of flower petals pressed into wet clay. This is more a garlanding of the well-heads but delightful all the same.
Painswick church is encircled by children clasping hands in the old Clipping Ceremony in September. This clipping has nothing to do with the yew trees in the churchyard, but comes from the Old English word meaning 'clasping'.
Marshfield's group of Mummers perform their age-old play on Boxing Day each year – in the snow if necessary.

Visitors to the Cotswolds

The Cotswolds as yet do not suffer in general from the tourist pressures experienced in places like the Lake District, Snowdonia and the West Country. In the West Country, tourists are sometimes known as 'grockles' – a term which implies that they, the visitors, are coming to make life worse for us, the locals. It is a pity that the scenic and commercial attractions of parts of our country can create pressures which provoke an adverse reaction. Ideally then, visitors should treat the places they visit thoughtfully and leave them unmarked, as though they had never been there.

Most people do. They do it by making an effort to understand the life of the place. They avoid walking through a field of corn or mowing-grass four abreast because it reduces the crop and the farmer's income. They remove all traces of their picnics. They admire drystone walls and think of the sweat, toil and skill which erected such cattle- and sheep-proof barriers. They do not climb over them nor take chunks for souvenirs or rockeries, even if the walls are decaying.

Occasionally, they whisper a momentary thank-you to the unknown people who put a footbridge in, built a stile, opened a pub, filled a pothole, trimmed a hedge, made a lay-by, put up the signposts – and are patient when they have to drive slowly for a mile behind a muck-spreader! In other words they follow the short country code:

Take nothing but photographs
Leave nothing but footprints
Kill nothing but time.

To those with such an awareness and the capacity to slow down will come the reward of welcome and the parting farewell of 'Do come back' – over and over again.

The Ancient Cotswolds

The orchis, trefoil, harebells nod all day,
High above Gloucester and the Severn Plain.
Few come there, where the curlew ever and again
Cries faintly, and no traveller makes stay,
Since steep the road is,
And the villages
Hidden by hedges wonderful in May.

To the Gloucester poet, Ivor Gurney, the Cotswold landscape was a high edge, dotted with windswept copses, and threaded by remote valleys in which hamlets sheltered. Today we can look down from this edge on the towns and fields of the fertile Severn Valley.

The ancient view was very different. Pollen from the peat near the Severn suggests that the valley was heavily wooded between the Ice Ages until widespread clearances began about 2,000 BC. Among the trees there were clearings, confined perhaps to the banks of alluvial gravel, from which Old Stone Age flint tools have been recovered. After the last Ice Age, about 10,000 BC, the Cotswold uplands were more lightly wooded. Trees grew steadily thicker on the hills until forest clearance marked the beginning of farming and settlement a little before 3,000 BC.

Cairns and mounds

The most obvious relics left behind by these New Stone Age people are the long barrows, 70 of which lie in the central Cotswolds. These are huge cairns of stones, carefully built with internal passages, roofed chambers, and drystone-faced walls. Their construction is estimated to have taken as much as 15,000 man-hours each – a huge amount of labour in a society of subsistence farmers. Though bodies are found within them, they were not cemeteries as we would understand them, for the number of dead in each is normally small; nor are they, like the Egyptian pyramids, the revered tombs of kings, for the broken-up skeletons within them were piled together, to our

The interior of Hetty Pegler's Tump, named after the wife of a 17th-century landowner.

eyes with small respect. They were perhaps places of ritual, designed to preserve and control the powers of the mighty dead. Two are particularly worth visiting in this area: Belas Knap, a little to the south of Winchcombe, and Hetty Pegler's Tump, near Stroud; both are now low, grass-covered stone mounds, with narrow stone-roofed chambers entered by low passages. When newly built, they must have caught the eye of the traveller on the skyline, great gashes of white limestone as obtrusive as a motorway viaduct.

The people who built them had recently taken to farming. They were now settling down on the land and not just living off it by hunting and fruit- and berry-gathering. Once it was thought that they formed small communes, having only peaceful contacts with each other – the exchange of flint or hard stone for tools. Discoveries in southern England over the past few years have told a different story, for New Stone Age villages, long looked for, are now being excavated and are proving to be strongly defended. Near Birdlip on the Cotswold edge, in the Country Park at Crickley Hill, the final Stone Age settlement was fiercely attacked by men using flint-tipped arrows, and then burnt – houses, shrine,

The Cotswolds are dotted with Stone Age long barrows. Trees delineate this one at Coberley.

defences and all. Some of the five earlier villages on this site, too, may have suffered a similar fate, for each showed clear signs of burning.

Though their lives were beset by superstitions, our Stone Age ancestors were people who are recognisably modern – gathered into groups under leaders capable of commanding major building programmes, jealous of their rights, and envious of the possessions of others. It is striking that estimates of the dead buried in long barrows would allow no more than some 200 per generation for the whole country. Whoever these dead were – chieftains, priests perhaps most likely – they were a highly select group of individuals.

The Bronze Age and its barrows

Among the obscure terms which travellers will find on their maps is the word 'tumulus'. In most cases the visitor will find a low circular burial mound, a round barrow, often now capped by a small coppice of trees. Over 350 of these are known in the Gloucestershire Cotswolds. Some can be seen only from the air. Others, like those at Wyck Rissington near Bourton-on-the-Water or North Cerney barrow near Cirencester, remain obvious landmarks.

To a much greater extent than the Stone Age long barrows they lie in clusters. This is particularly clear in the groups near Lechlade and near Upper Swell, to the north-west of Stow-in-the-Wold. At Condicote, are the remains of a *henge*, a huge circular earthwork, which was used for rituals early in the Bronze Age (at about the time of Abraham), and both long barrows and round burial mounds appear to be concentrated around it.

Where they have been excavated these round barrows normally cover a cremation burial in a pit, with occasional subsidiary cremations dug into the mound. It is likely that they were the burials of prominent individuals, and the clusters may be the cemeteries of such people over several generations, but where they lived is one of the great mysteries of this period. Elsewhere in England a few small villages of circular wooden buildings belong to this age of round barrows. Nothing of the kind is yet known from the Cotswolds, and the old joke, that the Bronze Age never lived, still holds true in this area. But the profusion of barrows in the hills, and the scatter of Bronze Age axes, daggers and spearheads, turned up by chance by the plough, show that it can be only a matter of time before their villages are identified.

The age of hill-forts

The Cotswold edge bristles with the remains of fortresses, the majority of which belong to the Iron Age, from about 600 BC. Even in ruins they are impressive, enclosing areas up to 100 acres in extent. Their banks are now gently sloping, grass-covered mounds, but, below the turf, excavations reveal tall, vertical drystone walls, whose effect was accentuated by rock-cut ditches. Their interiors today are featureless, to the extent that some have thought of them as cattle enclosures. Those that have been dug, however, have produced the remains of round and rectangular timber buildings and of burning and destruction, which hints at the motives which led Iron Age

Ritual stone circle and sacrificial slab excavated by volunteers at Crickley Hill.

rulers to protect their settlements with massive defences.

Some hill-forts are very large. That on Nottingham Hill, north-east of Cheltenham, at over 100 acres is one of the biggest in the country. Nearby at Conderton near Bredon is a tiny affair of only three acres. It seems certain that they must have had different functions. The large enclosures were perhaps tribal and marketing centres, and corrals for cattle; the smaller ones were probably the fortified residences of petty chieftains. In some cases we can see that different shapes are due to differences in date. The single-banked forts at Leckhampton and Crickley are of the 5th century BC. The magnificent tiers of ramparts which surround the hill at Painswick Beacon are probably four centuries later, belonging to a time of increasing tension between tribes, as smaller groups were being swallowed up to form major tribes in the last few generations of independence before the Roman Conquest.

The hill-forts tell only part of the story. Many, perhaps most, of the inhabitants of Iron Age Britain lived in the unfortified villages and farmsteads whose circular houses and fenced enclosures are a regular feature on aerial photographs. On the ground they are almost invisible and rarely worth a visit, but when excavated they provide a fascinating picture of life during the last few centuries BC. One such settlement, in the gravel pits at Beckford near Tewkesbury, revealed a regular pattern of rectangular, fenced yards, which were arranged beside a street and contained the remains of houses, and of rubbish- and storage-pits. A few of these settlements owed their origin to some natural resource – iron ore or salt – but most were agricultural communities of a dozen or so families.

From these small beginnings tribal centres were developing into towns in the last few years BC and the first years of our era, and relics of the growth are preserved in the Cotswolds. At Salmonsbury beside Bourton-on-the-Water a large 56-acre enclosure was found to be densely occupied from the numbers of round houses discovered there. Sitting as it does on a low-lying gravel bank and not high on a hill, Salmonsbury gives the impression of an early town rather than a hill-fort. A little to the north of Cirencester, near the village of Bagendon, is a perplexing series of banks and ditches which cut off an area of huge size – about 500 acres. Digging here has revealed some scattered occupation and has shown that in one part of the site lay a mint, producing that novelty from the Continent – coinage. This suggests that the area was politically important, a tribal capital, and gives us our first evidence for the name of the tribe who dominated the Cotswolds – the *Dobunni*.

A glimpse of the wealth of the chiefs of this age was revealed by accident over 100 years ago, when quarrymen came across a richly-adorned female burial on Barrow Wake near Birdlip. The objects, now to be seen in Gloucester City Museum, included bronze bowls, a silver gilt brooch, a decorated bucket, and one of that splendid series of highly-ornamented bronze mirrors which have been found scattered across southern Britain and which belong to the last years BC or the first few years AD. The Birdlip lady must have been one of the highest rank in her society. Who she actually was and where she lived are both quite unknown, but she is among the first of the prehistoric peoples of the Cotswolds who have a shadowy sort of identity.

Epilogue

Almost the whole of mankind's past is prehistoric, and little is known from written sources about Britain until the Roman period, a mere 2,000 years ago. Our knowledge about the previous hundreds of thousands of years of development and change has increased to an astonishing degree thanks to the careful investigations of the last two or three generations. We can now hold an axe made 50,000 years ago, or stand in the roadways of a defended village of the New Stone Age 5,000 years old, or touch the charred grains of barley last seen by an Iron Age farmer when he put them into his granary in 500 BC. Trade, warfare, and social relations may be guessed at by looking at the debris of the past, but, to an extent that historians and others accustomed to the written word find hard to imagine, the people themselves elude us.

Much of mankind's life is built on hope and its richest experience enhanced by story and song, but as far as prehistoric peoples are concerned their motives and hopes are lost, and we can hardly even imagine what they really felt when, like us, they stood in their then newly-built settlements on the Cotswold edge and gazed across the broad vale of the Severn.

The delicately-engraved bronze Birdlip Mirror, crafted during the Iron Age and now in Gloucester City Museum.

The Cotswold Countryside

A stonechat pauses with a beakful of food. These handsome birds prefer uncultivated land.

Origins

While the wide range of wildlife and scenery in the hills is the result of a variety of influences, the most fundamental of these is that of their geological structure. Some 180 million years ago the area we now know as the Cotswolds was under a shallow sea. For several millennia sediments composed of clay, sand and shell fragments were deposited on the sea floor and these accumulated to form the limestones that give us the hills of today. The famous oolitic limestones (so called after the spherical grains, or oolites, of which they are composed) form some of the finest building stone in the country and contribute to the special character of the Cotswold villages, farms and drystone walls. Some of the rock layers are highly fossiliferous and provide a clear indication of the prehistoric fauna and flora of the Cotswolds.

The relief of the Cotswolds is dominated by its steep scarp slope in the west. The highest point is at Cleeve Hill, north of Cheltenham, where 330 metres is reached. The gentle dip slope drops away to the south-east and it is here that many of the rivers rise and begin their course to link ultimately with the Thames.

Once the last ice sheets retreated some 10,000 years ago, plant and animal life began to colonise the hills. The natural vegetation of the Cotswolds would undoubtedly have been deciduous woodland, a very different landscape from that of today. As soon as human beings arrived, in Neolithic times, clearings were made in the forest. With the ensuing evolution of agriculture and growth of the population more and more of the woodland disappeared, giving way eventually to extensive tracts of rough grazing land. Changes continue to the present day and over recent decades the sheepwalks have given way to a landscape of more intensive agriculture.

Habitats

The combined effects of geology, climate, topography, soils, land-use history and present-day management give rise to the variety of habitats and wildlife that epitomise the Cotswold countryside. Farmland predominates with its acres of wheat, barley, oats, oil-seed rape, vegetables and grass leys (seeded pastures). Interspersed between the fields are tracks, hedges, walls and verges, all providing cover and food for their own range of wildlife.

Most woodland is concentrated on the steep slopes of the scarp. Elsewhere, on the dip slope the woods are smaller, though with some notably large exceptions, such as the forests of Chedworth and Withington, and Cirencester Park. Individual trees too are important in the landscape – they are the home of small wild animals, act as shelter for livestock and also have value as timber. Thickets of thorn, rose and elderberry grow on some of the steeper pastures and provide feeding, roosting and nesting sites for birds such as yellowhammer and stonechat.

Here and there, remnants of the once widespread sheep pastures remain, unaffected by plough, herbicide or artificial fertiliser. These famous Cotswold grasslands support a wealth of wildlife.

The young of the yellowhammer demanding food. The female builds the nest of dried grass and lines it with finer grass and hair.

Some of the Cotswold valleys are dry, indicative of an earlier, wetter climate, while others have small clear streams flowing through them. In some places, for example near the village of Barnsley, the stream is a winterbourne, flowing only in the winter when the water-table is high. Associated with the streams and springs may be small patches of marshy ground; where left undrained these support a variety of sedges and rushes, attractive flowers like marsh orchids and the amphibious frogs and toads.

Cotswold woodlands

Several different types of woodland habitat are to be found on the Cotswolds – old and new, broadleaved and evergreen. Surviving stretches of the ancient forest are found most frequently on the steepest hillsides. Although managed for timber they retain a truly native woodland vegetation and are the richest woods for wildlife. Beech, ash and oak are the commonest trees, complemented by yew, cherry, whitebeam, sycamore, holly and hazel, to name just a few. The forest floor is a patchwork of plants, sometimes carpets of bluebells, elsewhere extensive sheets of dog's mercury with its tiny green February flowers, or drifts of white ramsons scenting the air with garlic. Primroses are found along the tracks and are accompanied in spring by the delicate flowers of the wood anemone and wood sorrel.

Badgers are still common in the woods, although with their shy nocturnal habits are rarely seen. Fallow deer inhabit some of the larger woods, while the grey squirrel is ubiquitous. Foxes, small mice and voles add to the mammalian fauna of the woods.

Bird life can also be rich and varied, particularly where there is a good mixture of tree and shrub species and different ages of vegetation. Woodpeckers, titmice and finches

A tawny owl carries its prey back to its nest in the hole of a tree. It feeds on small mammals – mice, voles, young rats and shrews.

may be abundant and in springtime the air is filled with the songs of warblers such as chiff-chaffs, blackcaps, garden and wood warblers. There are winter visitors to the woods too, notably the large flocks of brambling from Scandinavia, which come to feast on the fallen beech mast (seeds). Tawny owls, sparrowhawks and buzzards may all be seen from time to time in the larger woods.

Cotswold grasslands

Once, the Cotswolds were dominated by rough grazing land, and even as recently as 50 years ago about half the area was under permanent pasture. Since the last War, however, there has been a dramatic reduction in the acreage of such land, so that today the ancient grasslands occupy but a tiny fraction of the overall area of the Cotswolds. These are either the steepest slopes of the valleys, impractical to plough, or the common lands, which, with their traditional rights of grazing held by local residents, have survived the agricultural changes taking place around them. Places such as Cleeve Common near Cheltenham or Minchinhampton and Rodborough Commons near Stroud include examples of this ancient, unimproved, calcareous grassland habitat.

Upwards of some 150 different species of grasses and flowering herbs may be found on a

Early purple orchids have long been associated with love and reproduction. They were used as a love potion and also for determining the sex of children.

Bird's-foot-trefoil is found in bright abundance on roadsides, pastures and grasslands.

single ancient common – the attractive quaking grass, purple thyme and knapweeds, yellow cowslips, rockrose, bird's-foot-trefoil and kidney vetch, white ox-eye daisies, blue harebells and scabious all combine to give a spangled beauty throughout the summer and autumn. The commons are famous too for their orchids – early purple and green-winged orchids in May, then bee, frog, fragrant, common spotted and pyramidal orchids in high summer.

Butterflies and other insects thrive on the diverse mixture of plant species and feed on the flowers. Specialities are the chalkhill and small blue butterflies, the marbled white and grayling. Common blue, green hairstreak, meadow brown and skippers are also resident, while visitors may

The peacock butterfly bluffs predatory birds by displaying its wings with their eye-like markings.

include the colourful peacock, painted lady and clouded yellow.

The key to the protection of these valuable grassland areas is their continued grazing by sheep or cattle to maintain their open character. Where there is insufficient grazing, shrubs like hawthorn, rose and dogwood encroach and could ultimately shade out the grassland flowers altogether. Thus in some areas scrub is cut back to ensure that a range of habitats is maintained and the maximum diversity of wildlife encouraged. At Painswick Beacon, for example, an unusual feature is the spread of Scots Pine across the once open hillside, and careful management is necessary to maintain the best areas of grassland while preserving some of the trees.

Rivers and streams

The main rivers of the Cotswolds – the Evenlode, Dikler, Windrush, Coln and Churn – rise from springs near the scarp and flow south-eastwards across the inclined plateau towards the valley of the Thames. The Thames itself rises in the Cotswolds, its source marked on the map at Thames Head not far from Cirencester.

The character of the streams owes much to the calcareous limestone over which they flow. Clear, sparkling water rippling over a stony bed is typical even in villages such as the Slaughters and Bourton-on-the-Water where the streams are an intrinsic part of the village scene.

Dragonflies and dainty blue damselflies are plentiful along the streams and alight on marginal reed grass and yellow flags. Long stretches of river are covered in summer with the attractive white flowers of the water crowfoot, a member of the buttercup family, while the banks may be overhung with alder and sallow. Otters once frequented the streams but have now sadly died out. Just occasionally one may be sighted journeying through the area, but more commonly nowadays it is mink which are spotted along the rivers.

Cotswold Water Park

By far the most extensive wetland area in the Cotswolds is the series of 100 lakes lying in two distinct areas south and east of Cirencester at the foot of the hills. The Cotswold Water Park is an entirely man-made habitat, the lakes having been formed as a result of some 60 years of gravel extraction in this uppermost part of the Thames Valley. Digging still continues, so more lakes are being created all the time. The area has become a major tourist attraction, and its wildlife coexists with those using the lakes for recreational purposes.

The alkaline nature of the water in the disused gravel pits is derived from the underlying calcareous limestone and gravel and gives rise to the characteristic features of such marl lakes – exceptionally clear blue waters, little algal growth and a diverse range of aquatic wildlife. The older lakes have become well colonised with marginal reeds and shrubs. Their wildlife interest is greatest where there are islands, inlets and shallow, shelving banks. Here may be seen nesting kingfisher, sedge warbler, mute swan and great crested grebes with their incredible spring courtship display. The willow beds of the Water Park remain a stronghold for nightingales, whose melodious song can be heard during the spring and summer.

In the winter the Water Park becomes a mecca for birdwatchers, who flock to watch the thousands of wildfowl which migrate here from the far north. Tufted duck, pochard, teal and wigeon are plentiful while smaller numbers of shoveler, gadwall, goldeneye and goosander may be spotted.

Other habitats

Away from the woods, pastures and streams, the farmland of the Cotswolds supports a wide range of wildlife. Birds such as corn bunting, partridge and pheasant have long been associated with the fields. Poppies still occur from time to time in cereal crops, and kestrels hover overhead in search of harvest mice in the wheatfields.

The drystone walls, so typical of the Cotswolds, themselves provide nooks and crannies for nesting wrens and robins. Ivy-leaved toadflax and English stonecrop root in the crevices, and lizards bask in the sun. Hedges too, with their scattered trees, give cover for nesting birds and food for the huge winter flocks of fieldfare and redwing.

Disused railway cuttings run through parts of the Cotswolds and present another habitat for fauna and flora. Old quarries too may be of interest not only to the geologist but also to the botanist – rare plants such as the limestone fern and Cotswold pennycress may be found on scree slopes. Even the old stone mines, with their horizontal shafts running underground, harbour wildlife. With their even temperature and humidity they are ideal sites for hibernating bats in winter, and some contain the very rare greater horseshoe bat.

Nature reserves

The Cotswold Commons and Beechwoods National Nature Reserve near Painswick includes some of the finest beechwoods of the Cotswolds and is easily accessible along marked public paths. The National Trust administers Minchinhampton Common and Rodborough Common, both near Stroud, and a number of other nature reserves are protected by the County Trusts for Nature Conservation and again cover a wide range of habitats. Woodland at The Frith (SO 875085), grassland at Swift's Hill (SO 877067), lakes at Whelford Pools in the Cotswold Water Park (SU 174995) and a stretch of disused railway track near Chedworth Roman Villa (SP 051138) are among the variety of attractive sites which serve to show the visitor the full beauty of the Cotswold countryside and its wildlife.

A kingfisher on its fishing perch.

Managing the Landscape

Shaped by history

Farmland near Dowdeswell. Before the 18th- and 19th-century Enclosure Acts this wold landscape would have been open sheep pasture.

The landscape which attracts us today is only about 150 years old. This is a very short period compared with the 6,000 years since human beings first started making an impact on the Cotswolds.

The first settlers were hunter-gatherers who moved into the area about 5,000–6,000 BC, but it was the Neolithic peoples who made the first impression on the landscape some 2,000 years later. They were the first farmers and carried out systematic clearance of the light, easily-cultivated soils of the hills to plant their crops. They left some 85 tombs to bury their dead.

During the Bronze Age the population increased and by the Iron Age, around 500 BC, there were many signs of occupation of the Cotswolds including some 35 known defensive sites.

The Romans left their permanent stamp on the landscape with their legacy of roads, two of which (Foss Way and Ermin Way) are still important through routes today.

When the Saxons moved into the area around the 7th century, they probably took over existing settlements on the Cotswold plateau and established new ones on spring lines with a ready supply of water. The majority of Cotswold place names have Anglo-Saxon origins, and, by the end of the Saxon era, much of the land was in the ownership of the Church.

By the time of the Domesday Survey of 1086, a large area of the Cotswolds was already under cultivation, with woodland along the western escarpment. In the following centuries more woodland was cleared, and the open field system of arable farming was increased until a maximum was reached in the 14th century. This period saw the real beginnings of the Cotswold wool trade and the area of sheep pastures was greatly increased, especially on ecclesiastical holdings.

After the Dissolution of the Monasteries in the 16th century, estates tended to be smaller. There was an upsurge in the building of Cotswold stone dwellings by country gentry and yeoman alike. The greatest landscape change occurred between 1700 and 1840 when at least 120,000 acres of open land were enclosed by Acts of Parliament. This gave rise to the familiar drystone walls and hedges dividing off the newly enclosed areas. Hunting and shooting became popular with the 'squirearchy' and many land-owners planted coverts and shelter belts for foxes and game birds.

Since the middle of the last century, the landscape has remained basically the same – predominantly agricultural, sprinkled with naturally integrated villages and farmsteads. In the last 40 years fundamental change has started again.

All these changes were made in response to needs felt by individuals, small groups, such as medieval merchants or a parish as a whole, big estates, municipalities or the whole nation. Food, shelter and warmth are vital needs. So fields were planted or grazed for food, trees felled and stone quarried for shelter, and more trees felled for warmth.

The methods appropriate to the time dictated how the land was used. Great sheep walks of scrub and grassland were managed by shepherds and their flocks. Woodlands were coppiced to ensure continuity of timber. Old field patterns with undulating ridge and furrow can be seen crossing the modern field boundaries. An ancient track can be detected by the way today's cornfield ripens earlier along its line.

Conservation and development

As the land was enclosed and formed into more efficient farming units to produce food more economically for an exploding population, so reaction set in on a national scale. There are now many organisations that aim to retain the traditional landscape. The following are a few examples.

The Open Spaces Society was founded in 1865 to retain as much as possible of the country's open space, such as commons, and make them available for public use. Thirty years later three far-sighted people formed a National Trust to acquire land as the only reasonably sure way of protecting it. Now, after nearly 100 years, it has vast property holdings and is the largest private landowner in the country. It is 'private' because it is not a government department. 'National' refers to its operation nationwide. It has many 'open space' properties in the Cotswolds open to the public at large without payment.

The Council for the Protection of Rural England was founded in 1926. It has fought on the political front on many occasions to ensure that major developments are carefully designed to blend into the countryside, or are even stopped if the apparent need can be proved to be false. Such developments are motorways, bypasses, airports, reservoirs, power stations, quarries and mines, as well as housing and industrial development in, for example, green belts.

The Ramblers' Association started in 1935 to preserve and enhance rights of way for the landless public. County naturalists' trusts were formed to acquire land for creating nature reserves. Of more recent foundation the Woodland Trust acquires woodland in order to preserve their existence and manages them to maintain a continuity of tree cover. Landowning and farming interests are also represented nationally by the National Farmers' Union and the Country Landowners' Association.

Governments altered the face of the land by creating the Forestry Commission after the First World War and charged it with producing timber to reduce our national reliance on imports. This was inevitably a long-term project and, equally inevitably, early decisions taken, such as planting quick-growing conifers, were criticised later when thinking and opinions changed. There are a number of Commission woods in the Cotswolds, but in a wider context it has a great influence on private landholdings by offering grants for suitable schemes.

The need in time of war for home-produced food moved governments into subsidising farmers, and this has gone further with the control of agricultural policy being determined on a European, rather than national basis. Introduce bigger and more efficient machinery and the farmer refashions the landscape by taking out hedgerows and drystone walls. Reduce farmers' milk production quotas and the landscape changes again to more corn, vegetables, sheep or oil-seed rape. Encourage him financially to 'set aside' cornfields because of over-production and he raises more sheep or woodlands. The profit motive drives farmers just as much as it does production and sales managers in factories. The landscape is a workshop – but what a nice one!

The pressures on the countryside over the last 90 years prompted a number of measures, for example the curbing of ribbon development of houses and industries along main roads between

towns. Eventually a more comprehensive approach was adopted in the Town and Country Planning Acts, and particularly in the National Parks and Access to the Countryside Act, 1949. This was later followed by the Countryside Act, 1968 and the Wildlife and Countryside Act, 1981. Apart from the creation of the Nature Conservancy Council and the registration of rights of way, 10 National Parks were set up, and other, less wild, places were designated as 'areas of outstanding natural beauty'.

In 1966, 582 square miles of the Cotswolds were so designated, and extended to 790 square miles in 1990. It is a compliment to the better side of human nature because most of the beauty has been fashioned by those who live and work here. Designation of an 'area of outstanding natural beauty' gives strength to local authorities to adopt policies intended to encourage sympathetic development.

Planning ahead

The task of planners is to reconcile many competing interests for the use of land. Builders would jump at the chance of erecting large numbers of houses in this very 'desirable area'; accessible to London and the south-east, the Cotswolds would also be attractive to industrialists wishing to open new factories. Motorways, reservoirs, quarries, oil exploration – cases can be made for all these in the interest of improving facilities and providing employment.

Main picture: Sheep grazing near Bisley. Inset: Old farm buildings are put to good use to house small industries, like this ceramics workshop at Northleach.

Tourism could be further developed with the provision of more hotels, caravan sites, zoos, funfairs and widened roads. On the other hand, farmers and naturalists alike may object to the restoring of a footpath because of possible vandalism – either to crops or to rare plants – by the newcomers it would attract.

Reconciling interests is made more difficult by the fact that there are 20 local authorities with territory in the Cotswolds – six county councils and 14 district councils. With so many people involved their views could well diverge and inconsistency result from different ways of treating development. To meet this a Joint Advisory Committee brings together local authorities and other interested bodies covering agriculture, tourism and conservation. This committee advises its constituent authorities on a common approach to problems and gives advice to developers, so that we do not destroy the very thing we wish to keep. From what may seem a boring 'dry-as-dust' committee atmosphere comes some protection of the view extending before you.

Major caravan developments have been refused. Rejection of an application for a zoo/ funfair resulted in a stately home being sold after being 200 years in the same family. Redundant barns house small industries as at Northleach, or convert to dwellings. Standards of house designs are improved to blend with the old, even if modern materials are used. Farming can be shown to be compatible with conserving wildlife and yet continue to be profitable. Farmers are encouraged to offer bed and breakfast accommodation and so use existing capacity to house tourists. New roads are 'landscaped' and verges are planted with trees appropriate to the Cotswolds.

In several ways the authorities are trying to cope with the pressures imposed by economics and by a more leisured and travel-conscious society. Some parts of the country suffer far more than the Cotswolds from the influx of visitors. Let us hope that this region will be able to absorb the pressures so that the delights illustrated in this book will be available for a long time.

Roman Roads, Towns and Villas

To the motorist travelling between the East Midlands and the Cotswolds, the Foss Way may be no more than a straight and convenient bypass to the main roads which pass through Coventry, Stratford or Cheltenham. The road is mostly narrow, often hilly, and quiet by comparison with its broad neighbours. Few may know that it was once the principal highway across the newly-conquered province of Britain.

Above: The Foss Way near Castle Combe. Opposite: Chedworth Roman Villa is a well-preserved example of Roman country life.

The Cotswold roads

Roman armies landed late in the summer of AD 43, probably at Richborough in Kent and near Chichester in Sussex. After fighting their way across the Medway and the Thames and subduing the tribal centre at Colchester and the great hill-forts of Dorset, they incorporated the south and south-west of England into a new Roman province. Some areas remained native princedoms, notably Hampshire under the 'king and ally' Cogidumnús. Part at least of the Cotswold Dobunni had, it seems, surrendered to Rome before the final overthrow of their allies, and a series of military works was soon built across their territory. Among the earliest were fortresses at Cirencester (soon to become a major city some two miles south of the Dobunnic tribal centre of Bagendon) and at Kingsholm near Gloucester.

The road through Cirencester to Gloucester is perhaps the earliest in the region and provided a rapid route from the southern ports, via the new town at Silchester south of Reading, onwards to Usk in Gwent, where an outpost fortress was built during these opening stages of the invasion. In its southern section, from Silchester to Newbury, this roadline has been mostly abandoned. Minor roads beside the M4 on the Marlborough Downs now continue its course to Swindon, where the A419, today on top of the Roman road, runs north-westwards to pass to the east of Cricklade and arrive at Cirencester. Now called the Ermin Way, the Roman road continues as the A417 across the Cotswolds to Gloucester. From Swindon onwards this is a fascinating stretch to drive along, for one can see the way in which the surveyors laid a straight course from crest to crest, sometimes continuing directly across to the next rise and sometimes altering the line a few degrees to bring the road nearer to its destination.

From the south-west the Foss Way (now the A433 and the A429) is aligned straight towards Cirencester, and then bypasses the town on what is now a tree-fringed lane, to meet Ermin Way between Preston and Siddington, originally the southernmost point of the Foss Way. The military road-builders obviously expected heavy traffic up from the south on Ermin Way, around Cirencester and then north-eastwards along the Foss across the rising hills of the Cotswolds towards the large native settlement of Salmonsbury at Bourton-on-the-Water. From there the road runs almost completely straight, over a distance of some 60 miles to the tribal centre that preceded the Roman city of Leicester. The end of its course, after a further 50 miles, was the legionary fortress of Lincoln.

Over recent years aerial photographs and excavations have revealed a series of small forts in the Midlands along the line of the Foss. In our region a possible candidate is the fort at Dorn, to the north of Bourton-on-the-Water. These forts date from early in the invasion period, and it is now clear that the Foss Way was intended to be the spine of a defence system between Lincoln and Cirencester, a spine which connected military bases and outposts both to the north and to the south. The scheme was not to build a fixed frontier, like that later constructed as Hadrian's Wall between the Tyne and Solway, but to create a broad military zone serviced by a fast road, the Foss Way, and cut by north–south roads radiating from the south-east. Behind the protected area, the pacification and Romanisation of the new province could proceed in safety.

Some of these other roads can be followed most easily on foot, or by the motorist content to tolerate detours where modern lanes pursue their own paths. The best to follow is perhaps Akeman Street. This ran from St Albans to form the main east–west street of Cirencester. Through most of its length in the Cotswolds it survives as short pieces of minor road. A stretch of its original Roman bank can be seen where it crosses the River Leach, by a footpath through fields a little over one mile to the north of the village of Eastleach Turville. To the south-west of Cirencester its line was continued by a later extension of the original Foss Way, and now forms a modern road (A433) to Kemble Airfield. Beyond the airfield it remains as a footpath along the boundary between Gloucestershire and Wiltshire, on its way to the Roman city of Bath.

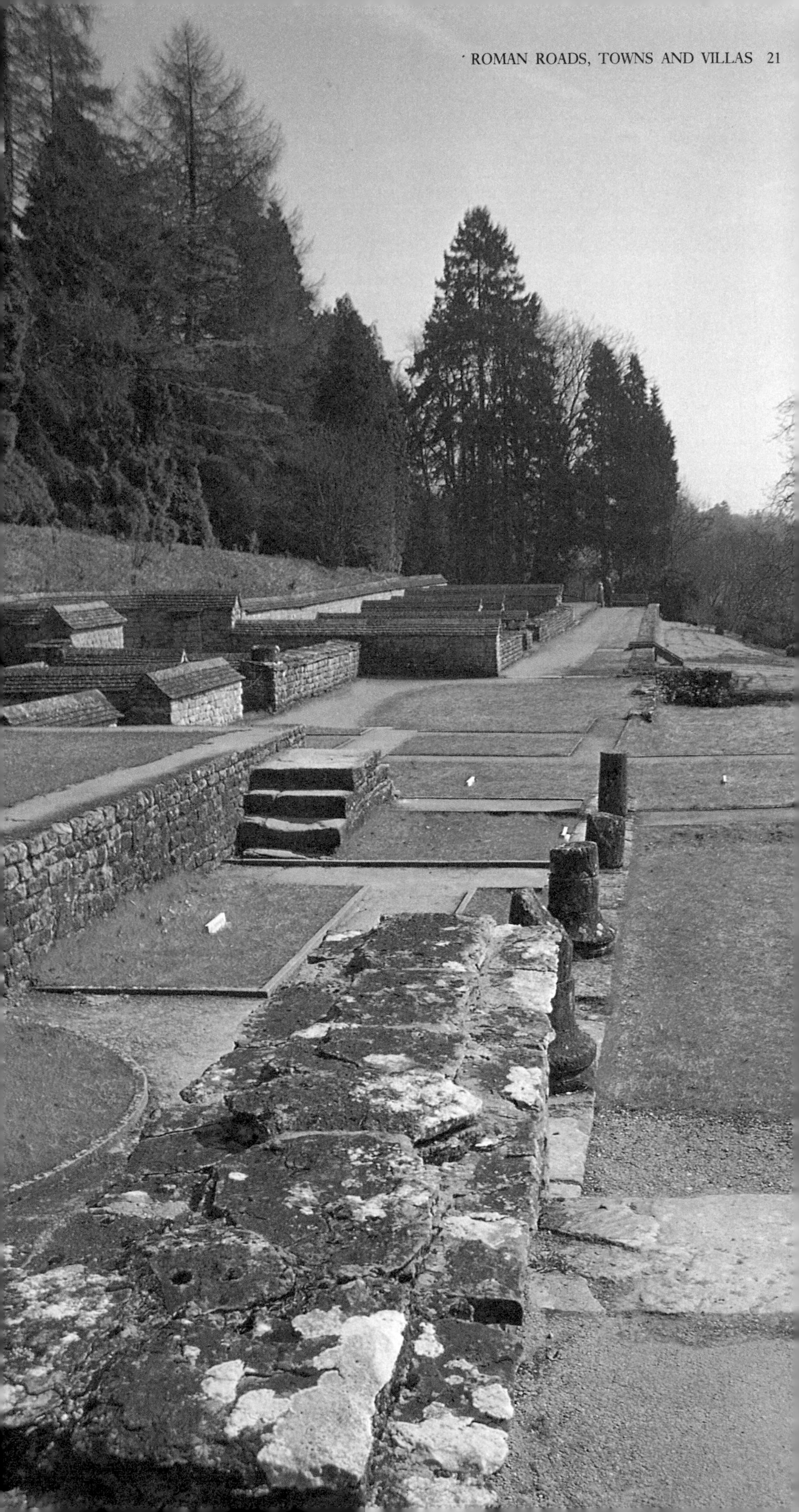

The Foss Way zone survived for little more than a decade, for Roman governors were forced by uprisings to press on into North Wales, northern England and, finally, 40 years after the invasion, into Scotland. But the later history of the province indicates the soundness of the initial choice. There were important Roman cities to the north of the Foss – Wroxeter, Chester and York. There are fertile agricultural areas with substantial country houses in the Midlands and the Vale of York. But the bulk of the native tribes, which were politically centralised and were already absorbing civilised Mediterranean practices, lay to the south of the Severn–Trent line, and, in the main, the villas and well-ordered countryside of the Roman period were to be found in this same area. Once across this early zone and into the Pennine foothills, the land, 300 years after the invasion, was still to be dominated by military bases.

Roman towns

The Roman statesman and historian, Tacitus, a contemporary of the British conquest, took a prejudiced view of the process of Romanisation. 'They create a desolation,' he said, 'and call it civilisation.' But Tacitus admired the noble savagery of the northern Barbarians and lamented its passing, and there is little sign that the natives saw the new styles of life in so gloomy a way.

In the Cotswolds the principal town was Cirencester, and a great deal of digging has revealed much of its early history. After the removal of the troops northwards to deal with the natives in Wales, the village which had grown up outside the fort was replanned on the largest scale. The administrative centre with its great hall was the largest civilian complex we know of outside London, and the final size of the town – at about 240 acres some two-thirds that of London – rivalled that of the greatest cities in north-west Europe. Outside the town lay a massive amphitheatre, imposing even in its present ruin.

As was normal, despite its importance, Cirencester was at first without defences, until in the later 2nd century some sense of insecurity (still only dimly understood) prompted the citizens of many Roman towns to begin the long task of enclosing themselves first in earthworks and then in masonry walls. Within, the town was divided into 15 street blocks, some parts of which have now been examined. Here, as in other Roman towns where excavations have revealed a large tract of the urban area, what is remarkable is that luxurious town houses are numerous. We must conclude that the urban population was disproportionately wealthy. Our model of the Romano–British town should not be industrial Birmingham, but Hampstead, Welwyn or Regency Bath. Its inhabitants presumably included a high proportion of the native nobility, not living now in the great wooden roundhouses of their old tradition, but in stone and timber mansions, decorated with painted plaster and mosaic floors.

The country houses

The town houses resembled the most striking feature of the Roman countryside, the villas. A wealthy man would own at least two properties – one in the town, and the other in the country not

far from the city – as the 4th-century writer, Ausonius, said, so that he could pass from one to the other at whim. A recent study of Roman Britain has demonstrated the point: the larger the town, the more numerous were the villas which were scattered within easy reach; the further one goes from a town, with few exceptions, the fewer country houses are to be found.

Cirencester, as befitted its importance, is the centre of a wide band of wealthy villas. Half the known mosaics from Roman Britain are in the south-west, and a very large number of these have been found in the Cotswold villas. Grandest of all is the palatial Woodchester, beside Stroud. The enormous complex extended over more than two acres and centred on an elaborate series of state apartments richly decorated with mosaics, some of which are periodically unearthed for display. Another, well worth a visit, is Chedworth, some six miles north-east of Cirencester, a little smaller than Woodchester but highly ornamented. A particularly fine example, somewhat smaller in scale, has now been opened to view at Great Witcombe near the Ermin Way south of Gloucester.

Even the greatest of the villas was clearly used in part for agriculture. The outer courtyards of Woodchester and Chedworth probably contained barns and similar buildings. In the smaller villas, such as Barnsley Park, the barn stands close to the house and paddocks encroach on the walls of the main building. At the lower end of the scale agricultural need predominated and the building was no more than a substantial farmhouse with few social pretensions.

Away from towns and from rural marketing centres, the rural population continued to have a life-style similar to that of their Iron Age forebears. Important work on the gravels around Lechlade has shown a steady development of a series of Iron Age farmsteads. Some, which

The Four Seasons mosaic pavement, now on display at the Corinium Museum, Cirencester.

developed during a prosperous period, may include a wayside shrine; later ones consist of a small but Romanised farmhouse and outbuildings. The sites, their information salvaged during gravel extraction, are unfortunately not now visible, but they stand as an exemplar by which we can understand the hundreds of small Romano–British native settlements recorded only as marks on aerial photographs. It was by the labour of the inhabitants of innumerable such places that the rich landowners were able to build these massive villas and prominent public buildings, which today survive as a monument to an elaborate, imported way of life.

The end of Roman Britain

From the middle of the 3rd century onwards the Roman Empire passed through civil wars, reconstructions, barbarian incursions, and finally began to fall apart through the great Germanic invasions of the 5th century. There is little sign of these traumatic events in the Cotswolds. In this period Cirencester grew in importance. About AD 300 it was chosen as the capital of one of the provinces into which Britannia was now divided and probably received the governor and his entourage. The local villas prospered, and the 4th century is the great period of elaboration of the Cirencester school of mosaics.

Both Gloucester and Cirencester remained urban centres into the 5th century. Recent work in the centre of Gloucester has shown that the forum, site of the town's administration and market, may have been turned over increasingly to industry and housing, and stone buildings were being erected after AD 370. At Cirencester the forum was being repaired well into the 5th

century. But by now their official function was obsolete, for Britain was independent of the Empire, abandoned as a dispensable outlier of Europe at a time when barbarian Visigoths and Vandals were striking into Gaul and Italy. The new rulers of the province were the local notables, probably ultimately of native origin, who may even have been the far descendants of the Celtic nobles of pre-Roman Britain.

Anglo-Saxon colonists by the middle of the 5th century were occupying parts of eastern England, and Roman patterns there were fast disappearing. No documentation exists for the Cotswolds, but at Withington, six miles south-east of Cheltenham, a strong case has been made for continuity from a Roman villa estate to a medieval village. Other estates near Winchcombe may have developed similarly, and at Frocester near Stroud excavations have demonstrated the conversion of the villa into a complex of timber buildings, presumably a chieftain's residence of this period. The Roman buildings did not always survive–the villas became dilapidated and were abandoned in favour of native houses. The Romano–British were reverting to the pattern of the Celtic, Iron Age past; their town councillors became noblemen, the strongest became hereditary rulers, and the royal palaces may well have been

Coin of Agrippa, Corinium Museum, Cirencester.

set up in the old town halls.

Very little is known of rural settlement in this time of change. Excavations at Crickley Hill have shown a huddle of stone and turf houses tucked behind the ruined rampart of the hill-fort. It seems to have been a small peasant village. But a couple of hundred yards away on the same hilltop a palisaded enclosure contained more substantial buildings, and seems to have been the home of someone altogether more powerful, perhaps a local noble whose ancestors occupied one of the several small villas in the plain beneath the hill. The return to Iron Age patterns is clear, and the towns, their function as centres of civilisation and Roman administration gone, withered away. In Gloucester a layer of black soil, probably from fields, overlay the ruins of the Roman buildings. At Cirencester the amphitheatre outside the walls may have been restored as a strongpoint. Elsewhere the Roman world passes into oblivion, until the first record of the new Anglo-Saxon overlords. At Dyrham near Bath, in 577, Saxons killed three British kings and then captured the three principal towns of the Cotswolds – Bath, Cirencester and Gloucester.

Cotswold Villages

How often have I paused on every charm,
The sheltered cot, the cultivated farm,
The never-failing brook, the busy mill,
The decent church that top the neighbouring hill . . .

Oliver Goldsmith's description of Cotswold villages still rings true 200 years after he penned these lines.

There are few towns on the Cotswold hills; all are country market towns grown up on the Cotswold wool trade – Tewkesbury, Cheltenham, Gloucester and Bath are of the vales. It is, therefore, the 200 or so villages that are the heart of the Cotswolds; a handful trade as towns, others are hardly hamlets – all are woven into the tapestry of the landscape.

Variety in the vernacular

The style in which the Cotsaller built his simple cot to shelter his sheep on the high and rolling wolds (hence the name 'Cotswold'), his humble home, his monastery's tithe barn, his lord's manor and his Maker's church was imposed by purpose rather than by design.

Long before the Roman invasion the local stone was quarried, cut and used for building. The stone lintels, walls and chamber roofs of the Neolithic burial site of Belas Knap on the high plateau above Cleeve Hill are witness to the skill of the early mason and the durability of the stone. The Romans built carefully planned towns in their own distinctive architectural style and enriched their country villas with mosaic pavements of great artistic design, but the walls of their rural estates and the *tesserae* (small stone or clay cubes used in mosaics) of their murals were of Cotswold stone.

The Saxons were farming folk and settled their communities on the hillsides and in the valleys, on wide open wolds and in secret, wooded combes. Their domestic buildings were mainly of timber and thatch, but most of their churches were of stone. Saxon *long-and-short work*, where broad horizontal stones alternate with narrow vertical ones on the corners of a building, survives in a few churches, as do isolated examples of their carving – crude in comparison with the precision of the Romans and primitive by Norman standards. The church at Daglingworth has fine cable mouldings carved on the doorway, and above it is one of the finest Saxon mass-dials (to indicate the time for mass) in the country. Prudent use has been made of a Roman stone altar – upended and pierced through, it becomes two tiny windows in the vestry wall. Saxons at neighbouring Duntisbourne Rouse used Roman stone coffin lids as seats inside their church porch.

Almost all the villages in the Cotswolds were established by the time of the Norman invasion. Few are not included in the great Domesday census, so most villages can claim Saxon roots.

The conquerors set about their building with vigour, and Gloucestershire is rich in surviving Norman church architecture, but it is the medieval builders who left the Cotswolds their great heritage. They built manor, farm, barn and cottage on a basic design: an essential principle of solid foundations, sturdy walls and roofs steeply pitched to carry the weight of the tilestones.

Cotswold stone itself brings variety to the buildings of the region; the varying degrees of mineral iron in the limestone strata account for differences in the colour of the stone. North wold quarries produced the honey-coloured stone found around Chipping Campden, Broadway and Stanton. Iron-rich rock gives Stanway its burnished gold distinction and is used to such striking effect to face the starkly simple lines of Prinknash Abbey close to Cranham village – quarried at Goscombe it is generally known as Guiting stone. Quarries of the central wolds produce a pearly-white stone; those in the south tend towards a soft grey.

Variations on the basic style evolved as a result of increased prosperity, reflected in size, stature and embellishment. Schools of local masons who knew their native stone, quarried and built with it, mostly to their own designs, raised domestic architecture to become the classic Cotswold style, copied in part or whole over the entire region. Church and barn, manor-house, cottage, pigsty and privy would have come from the same quarry; the same handful of masons would have raised the walls and laid the *slats* (tiles) on the high-pitched roofs, and the village blacksmith would have wrought the hinges, knobs and latches. So each village evolved with its own identity, all of a piece.

Buff-coloured stone houses in Little Rissington on the grassy Cotswold uplands (main picture) contrast with the timber-built style in the rich farmland of the Severn plain (below left).

Placenames

Cotswold placenames are essentially English. With the exception of Gloucester, Cirencester, and Frocester, which keep to their ancient Romano-British roots, the majority are derived from the Anglo-Saxon tongue.

A study of the placenames is fascinating and absorbing. Mainly they are straightforward statements of siting or shape with sometimes an early patron's name appended. Topographical features appear, as in Stow-on-the-Wold and Bourton-on-the-Hill, Wotton-under-Edge and simply Edge along the escarpment, and Winchcombe, Rendcomb and Stinchcombe indicate their positions in a cove-like valley, or combe.

Fords, wells, springs and brooks are indicated in such names as Burford, Fairford, Westwell, Broadwell, Seven Springs, Fulbrook and Swinbrook. Many villages beside a river form groups: twins, triplets and even quadruplets from parent stream or brook are affectionately known as The Ampneys, The Swells, The Colns – like families, and each, like different members of a family, has individual characteristics. Their upstream or downstream position is the usual forename, so Upper Swell and Lower Swell; the ancient form of *nether* for 'lower' retained only in Nether Westcote. Composite names often embody both direction and base, as in Northleach and Eastleach on the River Leach.

Saxon *cot*, variably spelt as *cott* or *cote*, meant 'cottage', giving a clue to that village having grown from smaller roots than one that ends with *ton*, from Saxon *tun* meaning 'farmstead'. Cotswold dialect has given colour and cadence to the basic components and altered many sounds. 'Farmstead by the pool' has been reversed and comes down the centuries as Poulton, pronounced 'polltun'. More difficult to recognise is the River Churn in North Cerney and South Cerney, and *stan* for 'stone', as in Stanton and Stanway, but the most deceptive must be the Shiptons, for they owe nothing to nautical ships and everything to the old Cotsaller's pronunciation of 'sheep'.

The shape of the villages

Three major factors decided the initial siting of the early villages: good water supply, fertile land and strategic defence positions.

Villages fall into two basic types: the manorial village, of either a monastic or a feudal lord, in which the houses are grouped round a nucleus of church, manor and farm, as at Notgrove; and the trade route village, which developed on a straggling street plan, as at Barnsley on the old Welsh Way.

Another distinct feature of the village pattern is the village green. A central grassed area where the community's stock could be herded together was essential in the days of marauding invaders and unenclosed fields. Some were mapped out by the manor as a common pulpit for notices and an open court where villagers could witness the rough justice meted out to their fellows in pillory or stocks. Other greens are an inheritance of ancient common rights where cattle can still graze. A pump, pond, or more anciently a well, served both as watering-place and meeting-place – a practice as old as the Scriptures.

Broadway, the show village of the north Cotswolds, is an example of how an original manorial grouping retains its identity while allowing development to extend along the main street. The green is large; the north side is backed by a line of buildings showing the features typical of fine Cotswold architecture – high gables, stone-tiled roofs, steeply pitched with dormer windows, tall and ornate chimneys. A timber-framed black and white house makes due acknowledgement to its Worcestershire roots and adds interest to the overall scene. The Abbot's Grange on the west side dates back to the early 14th century and is the oldest domestic building in the county. As manorial ties weakened, trade strengthened in the coaching era and the village developed on the broad way stretched out east of the green.

Spa Cottages on the Lower Swell to Stow road. A mineral spring was discovered here in 1807.

Development and decline

Broadway, despite its rapid growth, is still a village, as is Bourton-on-the-Water. Both are rooted in antiquity; both have developed on the tourist trade. Other villages which outgrew their manorial origins obtained the rights to hold a fair and a charter for a market early in their history and a number developed as small market towns.

The wool trade of the Middle Ages gave borough status to some 30 villages of the hill country alone; those that survived the decline of the wool industry did so only if they were well sited on developing traffic routes and formed a trading centre for a rural catchment area.

Close proximity to a larger borough meant the decline of some medieval towns. Blockley, though still busy and adapted to changed economies, never developed on the same lines as its neighbours Moreton-in-Marsh and Stow-on-the-Wold; Guiting Power reverted to a quiet village as Winchcombe grew. Prestbury became an adjunct of Cheltenham, and Churchdown and Whaddon down in the vale were swallowed up in the growth of Gloucester as a city.

In a few isolated cases it was the chance of fate which decided the future of the village. Maugersbury in the north was an established trading centre by the 12th century, but Henry I decreed that a borough should be created close by, where the ancient Cotswold ridgeway met the Roman Foss Way – a prime point on an arterial route. The resulting Stow-on-the-Wold prospered as a town; Maugersbury remained a village.

On the outskirts of the village of Lower Swell on the road to Stow is a cottage with an inscription stating that a chalybeate spring was discovered there in 1807. The neighbouring cottage was built as a spa but was never exploited. If it had been, the development of the north and central Cotswolds would have taken a quite different direction, with a spa town instead of a

A row of cottages at Broadway with their bay and dormer windows and steep gables.

Morris men at Chipping Campden.

tiny Cotswold village – a town averted and a village saved.

Culture and tradition
Deep-rooted tradition is welded into the culture of the Cotswolds. Sadly, the strong dialect is fast disappearing under the influences of newcomers and television; what remains is, therefore, all the more worth preserving. However, more tangible than local idiom is local custom.

The Cotswold calendar is punctuated by events renewing ancient ties to the cycle of seed-time and harvest, the dying of the old season and resurrection of the new. So tightly woven into the pattern of village life are these customs that pagan ritual has been absorbed into the fabric of Church tradition.

The pretty village of Randwick in the Painswick valley is an enclave of ancient custom: early in May is the cheese-rolling round the church and the curious mayor-making ceremony, known as the Randwick Wap.

Whitsuntide – now Spring Bank Holiday – sees the continuance of Robert Dover Games and the Scuttlebrook Wake at Chipping Campden, cheese-rolling down the precipitous Cooper's Hill, and Woolsack Races up Tetbury's steep Gumstool Hill.

Well-dressing is a pretty blessing in the little hill village of Bisley on Ascension Day, and, still in the Stroud valley area, the villagers of Painswick encircle their church hand in hand in the Clipping Ceremony in mid-September.

Christmas-tide brings out the Mummers to re-enact the complex ritualistic fight of good conquering evil, interwoven with primitive fertility rites.

Morris men dance their colourful way through the numerous feasts and festivals, fairs and village fetes, announced to all by the Cotswold Town Criers.

The annual fairs, such as Stow Horse Fair and the 'Mops' originated from the statute and hiring fairs, trading under centuries-old charters. The hiring fairs were the forerunners of the employment exchange where workers offered themselves for hire, each wearing a token of his calling – the carter a twist of horsehair in his hatband, the shepherd a lock of wool on his smock.

Village life today
In a strange way it is the affinity with the past that bodes well for the future of this quiet corner of rural England.

Villages depopulated in Victorian times, as new factories drew depressed communities to work in the developing towns, are fast becoming re-settled. The attractions of the Cotswolds are manifold. The temperate pace of a village is both a novelty and a salve to those subjected to the hurly-burly and pressure of city life, so it is often a haven for the retired or a weekend retreat for young families. While this is understandable, it is also easy to see that too great an influx of newcomers, whether transient or resident, could so quickly destroy the very qualities that attracted them there in the first place.

Craftwork has been greatly revived in recent years and helps to continue a tradition as well as to provide work in the locality. The watchful eye of a trust such as the one at Stanway and Guiting Power helps to conserve the best of the past and integrate it successfully with the demands of the present. A village must be a living entity, where villagers care for and about their village, preserving its character created over many generations.

The Cotswold Way

The Cotswold Way offers views of more than the Cotswolds to its walkers. As a scarp path there are views far and wide to the south, west and north, across the vales to hills and mountains beyond. About 100 miles long, it was conceived in the 1950s by the Gloucestershire Branch of the Ramblers' Association. The National Parks and Access to the Countryside Act, 1949, provided for the registration of footpaths and gave government support (and money) for the creation of long-distance footpaths. The Cotswold Way was submitted for consideration but did not achieve recognition (or money) and so was shelved. In the late 1960s Gloucestershire County Council revived the idea by sponsoring the Way as one of its countryside initiatives for European Conservation Year in 1970.

For two years a full-time warden supported by a number of volunteers and rambling clubs researched the detailed route. Formal inauguration in National Footpath Week 1970 took the form of various organisations officially walking a portion each.

The Cotswold Way is essentially a linking together of existing rights of way; it is not the resurrection of an ancient route. Inevitably there are gaps which have to be linked by walking along a road or making a large detour round areas where rights of way do not exist or cannot be negotiated. Although the efforts of dedicated volunteers have been enormously successful in filling these gaps and reducing road walking, eventually there has to be official involvement, particularly for diversions.

Volunteers, notably the Cotswold Voluntary Warden Service and the Ramblers' Association, have put in many hours of work to improve the physical standard of the Way. 'Operation Cotswaymark' started in 1975 to waymark the

entire route. This was no mean task and meant taking on 100 miles of landowners. A mile or two of permission was sometimes easy to achieve when it involved just the agent of a big estate; elsewhere one mile might involve a dozen owners.

Although the Highway Authorities have power to enforce waymarking, it was felt better, for the sake of relationships, to seek permission. Most landowners immediately recognised the value of waymarking. Not only does it give walkers a sense of security to know where they have a right to go, it enables farmers to direct those who have strayed back to the correct route.

The method of waymarking uses the Country-

Long-distance hikers enjoy the view from Crickley Hill.

side Commission system of coloured arrows, thus: yellow for walkers (footpaths); blue for horses, walkers and push-bikes (bridleways). This is a nationally recommended system available for use on footpaths and bridleways throughout the country. In addition a similar arrow in white has been used on roads (including unsurfaced ones), with the Cotswold Way denoted by a white spot near the arrow, to show the continuity of a through route. Other circuits of walks may have a different symbol near the arrow.

Ideally one should say goodbye to the car and walk the route in sequence, staying in local accommodation or in a tent. However, readers may wish to walk a section weekend by weekend, or stay at one or two places. If you go with friends, two cars can make the walk easy. Obviously, one car is parked at the end of the day's selected distance and the other transports the walkers to the start. If you are walking solo, a folding bicycle can be used to cycle from the car parked at the end point to the start. Conceal the bike if possible and lock it ready for collection at the end of the day.

You should be physically fit. You will climb 10,000 feet, though you will never be more than 1,050 feet above sea level. You should be well-

A Voluntary Warden places a yellow arrow to indicate a footpath for walkers. The Cotswold Way is now waymarked for its entire length.

shod in good walking boots giving firm support to the ankles. A sweater may be desirable, particularly if it is windy. It always feels several degrees colder on the hills than it does in the vale or in the sheltered places where you may be staying. Waterproofs are essential at most times of year. With luck, you may only need them for sitting on a mossy bank to eat your sandwiches.

To get the best out of the walk obtain one of the guidebooks currently available. Expect to walk no more than two miles an hour on average. Five or six hours' walking a day gives time to linger and explore. The Way has been walked by youngsters upwards of seven years of age, when the programme starts gently with, say, the first days adjusted to seven miles.

The prevailing wind is from the south-west (up the Bristol Channel and the Severn) and the sun runs to the south. So the Way is now considered as a south-to-north route with sun, wind and rain on your back, opposite to the original concept. Here is a 10-day itinerary starting in Bath.

Day 1 – 10 miles   Bath to Cold Ashton

One can think of the Way as a pilgrimage from the great abbey of Bath to the parish church of St James in Chipping Campden. In olden times pilgrims would put their affairs in order, make their wills and commit themselves to the care of the Almighty before setting off. Fortunately today you should be reasonably safe from highwaymen, hostile natives and bogs to swallow you up. The people you are most likely to meet are those who chose to walk the other way!

From Bath Abbey the Way winds through alleyways, past the Georgian elegance of Queen's Square and the Royal Crescent. The Royal Victoria Park, High Common, Primrose Hill and the northern outskirts of Bath lie before Weston 'village'. A charming church and a parade of old buildings give way to a modern development and then the first real entry into and ascent of the hills.

Glancing back towards Bath from Penn Hill, you take your final leave of the Avon valley from Prospect Stile near the racecourse. Northwards the first of 12 hill-forts is reached (Littledown), before the second golf course and the monument to Sir Bevil Granville, killed in the Civil War battle of Lansdown. Thence the Way winds from what was formerly Somerset into former Gloucestershire and the tranquil Hamswell valley before reaching the A46 and Cold Ashton. Opposite the famous Elizabethan manor, a more recent long-distance footpath, the Limestone Link, reaches the end of its journey from the Mendips.

Day 2 – 11 miles   Cold Ashton to Horton

Pennsylvania and Dyrham Wood precede the descent to a lower level reaching Dyrham village. Dyrham Park (National Trust) is open only from the A46 above. The Way follows the outside of the Park wall. Now with much of the stone removed, one can occasionally look into the deer park through the replacement fence. In 577 on the slopes outside the Park the West Saxons defeated the Britons in battle and drove them westwards towards Wales.

North across the busy A46/M4 junction, the Way diverts into Tormarton, passing from Wessex into Mercia. Although Dodington

House is concealed behind trees, the Way crosses farmland of the estate, the wealth of which was built on West Indian sugar plantations worked by negro slaves.

At Old Sodbury the sudden sound of trains marks the unseen western portal of a two-and-a-half mile tunnel on the London–Wales main line. Little Sodbury hill-fort is above the manor where William Tyndale had an early job before his great work of translating the Bible into English, for which he was burnt at the stake. The day closes by reaching Horton.

Day 3 – 9½ miles   *Horton to Wotton-under-Edge*
(*Chipping car park*)
The Way ascends the scarp to Hawkesbury Upton and the Somerset Monument, which you may climb for a view from an extra 120 feet up.

From the windswept heights and into the secluded Kilcott valley, the Way passes out of the modern county of Avon into Gloucestershire just before Alderley. A sunken gulley carries the route above Wortley to emerge with extensive views over Nanny Farmer's Bottom. The Cotswolds are full of bottoms!

Wotton is certainly under the edge of the scarp but still high above the vale. It is a friendly and lively working town.

Day 4 – 8½ miles *Wotton-under-Edge to Dursley*
(*May Lane car park*)
A brief exploration of Wotton can precede today's walk before climbing to the Jubilee clump of trees and into the National Trust's Westridge Woods.

The Way skirts Brackenbury Ditches hill-fort before reaching the Tyndale Monument. This tower can be climbed, provided you go down into North Nibley and come back up again with the key.

Again a sense of seclusion accompanies you whilst crossing Waterley Bottom. This is in contrast to the heights of Stinchcombe Hill where the route gives superb views as it follows the edge of the golf course before descending into Dursley.

Day 5 – 11 miles   *Dursley to Standish Woods*
(*Cripplegate/Shortwood car park*)
Industrial Dursley gives way to the upland of Cam Long Down. Local legend credits the Devil with creating this strange-shaped hill by emptying the contents of his wheelbarrow. Ask local people why!

The flanks of Uley Bury hill-fort are followed by Coaley Woods which have recently undergone considerable thinning. The intriguing name of Hetty Pegler's Tump describes the prehistoric barrow above. Frocester Hill and Coaley Peak

A panoramic view of Cam Long Down, as seen from Uley Bury.

Picnic Site give fine views of the wide sweeps of the Severn.

To avoid Stroud the Way crosses the River Frome, the Stroudwater canal and the railway west of the town, before the rise to Standish Woods.

Day 6 – 8½ miles *Standish Woods to Cooper's Hill (picnic area car park on A46)*
Haresfield Beacon and its hill-fort start the day before you enter the intimacy of beech woodland. The Siege of Cromwell's Stone seen here refers to the Civil War.

Leaving the scarp, the Way now visits Painswick set on its own promontory within its own valleys. The town deserves exploration as a gem of Cotswold architecture. There are some fine mill buildings associated with the cloth trade along the Painswick Stream (not actually on the Way).

Painswick Common, with its Beacon, lies to the north of the town and hosts another hill-fort, Kimsbury, and another golf course. Beech woodland takes over again as far as Cooper's Hill where the car park lies just below the Way.

Day 7 – 10 miles *Cooper's Hill to Leckhampton Hill (Salterley quarry car park)*
The Way coincides with the nature trail to the maypole and then diverges, taking an easier route than the cheese-rolling slope into Cooper's Hill village, which is on the contour of the hill. Witcombe Woods curve round to Birdlip and the Roman Ermin Way. A new route dedicated over Barrow Wake enables the walker to enjoy the same notable view over the Vale of Gloucester as the motorist in the huge lay-by above.

Crickley Hill Country Park offers woodland and archaeology trails before the Way moves towards Leckhampton Hill.

Day 8 – 11½ miles *Leckhampton Hill to Cleeve Common (quarry car park near golf clubhouse)*
Today the route follows the rim of an amphitheatre of hills above Cheltenham, broken by the valleys of the Lilley Brook and the infant Chelt.

Leckhampton Hill was quarried for stone to build Regency Cheltenham. The Devil's Chimney, just below the Way is a relic of this and has now been repaired to keep it as a notable landmark.

Passing through the gorse onto Charlton Kings Common, the route descends gently to Seven Springs. Strictly off the Way, just round the corner on the A436 Gloucester road, the Springs mark the source of the Churn, which, because it is the remotest source of the Thames and its tributaries, gives rise to claims to be *the* source of the Thames.

Now follows a mile of road walking which it is hoped to change one day. It can be avoided by

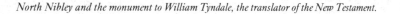

North Nibley and the monument to William Tyndale, the translator of the New Testament.

using tracks and paths further 'inland', but this adds an extra mile before rejoining the road before Ravensgate Common. Lineover Wood leads down to Dowdeswell Reservoir, from which the climb leads to open fields and the Happy Valley. This valley runs parallel with the scarp. The view is concealed, creating a secluded feeling before opening out to present Cleeve Common, the highest and the wildest part of the walk.

The hill-fort on the edge, however, boasts a golf course green actually inset in the rampart – to the displeasure of archaeologists. The Way passes through the golf course, with the wilder country being reserved for tomorrow.

Day 9 – 13 miles   *Cleeve Common to Stanton (car park at lower end of village)*
At this stage you should be fit enough to tackle the longest day. In these 13 miles the experience is of the greatest remoteness the Cotswolds can give, contrasted with the bustle of a country town. The eastern part of Cleeve Common is the nearest the Cotswolds come to the wild uplands of the National Parks. Even the farmland beyond gives that delicious excitement of being far from civilisation.

The long barrow of Belas Knap precedes the descent into Winchcombe. At Abbey Terrace the Cotswold Way is joined by the Wychavon Way completing its 40-mile course from Droitwich across the lush Vale of Evesham.

The altarpiece of St Michael's Church, Stanton, much refurnished early this century.

The Pilgrim's Way leads to Hailes Abbey. On the scarp at Beckbury Camp an ornamental seat is provided at Cromwell's Clump (Henry VIII's Thomas Cromwell this time). Legend relates that he witnessed the dismantling of Hailes Abbey from this point, but the trees have grown well in the last 400 years to conceal the view.

The final descent of the day reaches Stanway, with its great house, and leads to an amble across parkland and fields to Stanton.

Day 10 – 10 miles   *Stanton to Chipping Campden*
Stanton is a model of a Cotswold village restored to its present condition by the initiative of one man, Sir Philip Stott. The street carries the Way up the hill and gives a parting glance at the Guildhouse, a modern creation for learning and practising various crafts, built by another inspired individual, Mary Osborne.

The scarp walk continues with wide views on the way to Broadway in Worcestershire. Broadway draws the crowds. One can understand why and appreciate it despite them.

The climb to Broadway Tower is the last as the journey closes with a final sweep of the wolds before dropping down into the beauty of Chipping Campden.

The official end of the Way is by the Market Hall, but you may care to go a little further to St James's Church and give thanks for a safe arrival as requested in that prayer at Bath Abbey!

Guide books on The Way are available in bookshops, and for further information on accommodation contact: Cotswold Warden Office, County Planning Department, Shire Hall, Gloucester, GI1 2TN.

Stone-built houses overgrown with climbers at the delightful village of Stanton, sensitively restored by Sir Philip Stott.

Gazetteer

▲ Dovecote at Minster Lovell

Each entry in this Gazetteer has the atlas page number on which the place can be found and its National Grid reference included under the heading. An explanation of how to use the National Grid is given on page 76.

THE AMPNEYS

MAP REF: 94SP0801

Ampney brook never achieved the status of a river but has given its name to an area far beyond its headwaters. Ampney Down marks its northerly point as it touches the Roman Foss Way (A429), on the Cirencester to Stow road, with Ampney Sheephouse close to the Welsh Way where the old drovers took their herds on the hoof westward to Gloucester markets.

Ampney Crucis is the largest of the three Ampneys on the Cirencester to Fairford road. A turning off the main road by the Crown of Crucis inn leads over a bridge to a picturesque corner of old millhouse, minute village green, a trim little lodge house and an evergreen bower through which the ancient church is located. The fine churchyard cross and Holy Rood dedication of the cruciform church accounts for the Crucis.

Ampney St Peter, compactly grouped on a single street off the main road, has great charm in its simple style. Across the road to the south-east is Ranbury Ring, a Neolithic encampment.

The third of the Ampneys was wiped off the banks of the little brook by the Black Death. Ampney St Mary was rebuilt at Ashbrook, the 'east brook', really a stream tributary of the Ampney brook, some half a mile away to the north. Yew Tree Cottage garden is occasionally open as part of the National Gardens Scheme and is a superb example of a natural cottage garden. Of the original village only the little church remains in a field alongside the main road. Locally called the Ivy Church from the days when it stood in ivy-clad neglect, it is back in service today attracting attention to its medieval wall-paintings and bold Norman tympanum depicting a graphic moral of good conquering evil. It is an isolated, tranquil spot where only the sound of the brook breaks the silence as it goes on to complete the quartet with Down Ampney, some four miles away to the south.

▲ Great Badminton epitomises the typical English estate village.

BADMINTON

MAP REF: 78ST8082

Badminton is now synonymous with the grace and rigour of the famous three-day event held each spring. It is the oldest established horse trials and has been described as the toughest test of horsemanship in the world. Badminton has become a Mecca for horse-loving folk to thrill at the supreme skills of top-class riders in the company of the Royal Family.

The seat of the Dukes of Beaufort for some three centuries, Badminton was laid out on the most ambitious landscaping plan of all the Gloucestershire great estates. On the Tetbury to Bath road it is bounded by a five-mile avenue of glorious beech trees.

Great Badminton is a perfect example of an estate village; the almshouses bear the ducal arms and the broad street is trim and neat.

The parish church of St Michael is attached to the mansion house and furnished with classical monuments and exquisite sculptures of the Beaufort family. The most elaborate memorial, to the first Duke who died in 1699, was brought from the Beaufort Chapel at Windsor and necessitated the building of the chancel at Badminton to accommodate it.

Paradoxically, it is the small Cotswold stone-tiled church at neighbouring Little Badminton which is the private ducal chapel. Thatched cottages and farm

▼ The Ivy Church, as it is known locally, stands a lone sentinel to its past, marking the site of the medieval village of Ampney St Mary.

buildings cluster round the village green, a circular dovecote being its focal point.

THE BARRINGTONS
MAP REF: 91SP2013

Viewed from the high ridge road of the A40, Little Barrington settles like a toy in the broad valley below – the Windrush winking as it catches the noonday sun. The road descends between high shrubby banks and the little village opens out at the bottom.

Cottages cluster on raised paths around the village green as on the rim of a bowl, the humpy hollow providing the stone for their building. A trickle of a stream in the bottom keeps it green with tall wetland plants.

The church stands apart, on a side road. There is much Norman masonry in this mainly 14th-century building, including a clear cut tympanum on the north wall.

The Barringtons are synonymous with stone. Little Barrington was the home of the notable Strong family whose work under Christopher Wren took both mason and stone from this quiet Cotswold corner to rebuild some of the finest of London's buildings after the Great Fire.

The short stretch of road between the two low bridges is still known as Strong's Causeway after Thomas Strong, who laid the foundation stone of St Paul's Cathedral. Thomas left money to 'make a way between the Barrington bridges . . . to carry a corpse in safety'.

Great Barrington is an estate village. A very high wall encloses the park, its Palladian mansion of which Pope wrote 'at Barrington shall English Bounty stand', and the parish church.

MEDIEVAL LEGACY

If you stand in the market-place of a small Cotswold town like Northleach, surrounded by worn stone houses and dominated by its enormous church, or if you walk down the steep hill of Burford with ancient buildings crowding in around, then you may well have a strong impression of an unchanging medieval past. The reality is very different, for the old stone villages and small towns that dot the Cotswold landscape owe most of their form to the massive rebuilding that spread through the area after the 15th century.

▼ Great Coxwell Tithe Barn near Faringdon, Oxfordshire, dates back to the early 14th century.

In the early Middle Ages the landscape probably looked little different from its prehistoric pattern of dispersed farms and hamlets. The traveller through Saxon England would find some differences, of course. Churches would be the most obvious novelty, but for a long period there were only a few – monastic establishments in Gloucester, Cirencester, Tewkesbury, Winchcombe and Deerhurst. The parish churches which now form such notable landmarks belong to the replanning of the land which was going on in the last century or two before the Norman Conquest.

By 1250 at least 20 new boroughs had been founded in the area. Many, like Moreton-in-Marsh, Northleach, or Chipping Campden clearly had a small old centre to which was now attached a grid of new streets. We know a little about these places from excavations. Houses were at first single-storeyed, built largely of timber with stone foundations; streets were roughly cobbled, and the backyards were choked with rubbish pits.

Changes began in the later 13th century. With increasing prosperity because of the expanding woollen industry we find heavy investment in buildings. The most striking are the barns built by the major landlords to house their crops. Among the oldest, and as large as almost any in England, is Great Coxwell near Faringdon,

Oxfordshire. A similar monastic barn, at the other end of our region, is Bredon near Tewkesbury, now restored after a terrible fire in 1980. Both are well worth a visit, and the comparison between these magnificent structures and those rude peasant houses found in excavations underlines the vast gulf in medieval society between the rich and the poor.

Even prosperous houses were still built largely of wood. When we look at the medieval houses of Burford, all we can see on the street side is honey-yellow Cotswold stone. A survey of these buildings, however, has revealed that the stonework is a late façade applied towards the end of the Middle Ages. Behind the fronts stand the remains of timber-framed houses, improved and brought up to date by new fashions.

These fashions have left a permanent mark on the Cotswolds. Steep stone roofs, a profusion of gabled dormer windows, doorways decorated with flat pointed heads, and the characteristic rectangular drip-mouldings around the windows. Take a picture of a Cotswold scene, and its buildings will immediately identify it. This is the impression that the visitor will take away from the Cotswolds, a land of broad rolling fields and pasture, of narrow wooded valleys, of small stone villages and winding roads thick with hedges, wonderful in May.

BIBURY

MAP REF: 94SP1106

'The most beautiful village in England' was how William Morris described Bibury. Throughout history people have been drawn to this lovely spot in the central Cotswolds where the hills fold gently down to the Coln valley. Remnants of Celtic fields, an Iron Age hill-fort, a long barrow and beehive chamber with stone cupboards or niches are evidence of early settlement in the area.

The village itself centres on fine old cottages round a square on the north-west side of the church and must be sought out by a detour off the main road. St Mary's is rich in Saxon work and was held as a 'peculiar' by Oxfordshire's Osney Abbey until the Dissolution. The fine collection of sheep corbels pays tribute to the major part that wool once played in the life of the village.

In the same corner is Bibury Court, noble, gabled, and now a hotel, prettily situated on the banks of the Coln as it winds its way out of the village.

Across the river is Arlington Row. Backed by dark woods, the tiny cottages which once housed the village weavers are enchanting with their steep-pitched roofs and irregular forms touched with the patina of three centuries. The National Trust owns them and Rack Isle, the water-meadow on to which they face, a protected

▲ Blockley — one of the world's first villages to have electricity.

breeding ground for wildfowl. It takes its name from the time when it was a drying ground for cloth woven in the cottages and fulled at the mill opposite. Awkward Hill in the corner is steeply banked with more attractive cottages.

The Swan Hotel has long been famous as a fisherman's haunt and even earlier as a favourite rendezvous of the gay blades who flocked here for the Bibury Races of King Charles's day. The tiny windowless building close by was the old village lock-up.

Across the bridge is Bibury Trout Farm, covering some eight acres where visitors can catch their own rainbow trout, all bred in the crystal Coln river waters. Equipment can be hired and no particular angling skills are

required here. The impressive bulk of the 17th century Arlington Mill is the trout farm's neighbour. Now a folk museum, its 17 rooms are filled with the area's agricultural past, as well as boasting a charming William Morris room. The hamlet of Arlington, concentrated around its green high on a bank, joins with Bibury as the A433 angles off westward to Barnsley and Cirencester.

The minor road by the Swan Hotel follows the upstream course of the Coln valley. Ablington, the nearby hamlet, was the home of Arthur Gibbs, the young squire who immortalised it in *A Cotswold Village*, the first of the classics to look at country life with poetic insight.

Winson, up-river, also achieved literary notice as the home of Robert Henriques, author of *Through the Valley*.

▼ These cottages at Bibury are the quintessence of Cotswold domestic architecture: steep-pitched roofs and sturdy walls of native stone.

BLOCKLEY

MAP REF: 84SP1634

An administrative island of Worcestershire for 1000 years, Blockley was transferred to Gloucestershire in 1931 when many county anomalies were ironed out.

A large village, equidistant from Moreton-in-Marsh and Chipping Campden but not distant enough to develop into a market town itself, Blockley harnessed the water power of the deeply cleft valley early in its history.

Industrialised – albeit on a small scale by modern-day standards – and insular, Blockley has more of the Stroud valley character in its old mills terraced amidst the long rows of cottages along the steep and narrow ledges above the valley, than that of the north wolds village. But the golden glow of local ashlar stone and its architecture establishes its correct geographical identity.

Cheap labour in the aftermath of the agricultural and cloth trade depressions, and spring-studded hillsides made Blockley a prime choice for the silk-throwing mills based on the Coventry ribbon trade. A hundred years ago six mills employed some 600 people. The buildings have now been converted to other uses, but harmonise well with contemporary cottages and add character to an attractive village.

Blockley's former stature can be gauged by its church, which was large in Norman times, the busy High Street and the fine manors of Northwick Park and Upton Wold to the north and west. Blockley survived where others could not, for across and under the fields lie two deserted villages – Upton and Middle Ditchford, just a couple of the estimated 165 such lost medieval villages in Gloucestershire.

BOURTON-ON-THE-HILL

MAP REF: 84SP1732

An artist's delight is the steep street lined with cottages set prettily in terraced gardens, leading up to the lovely old church on the hill.

The rigours of the rise have been known to travellers from early times and Bourton on its hill was part of the turnpiked 'Great Road' from London and Oxford to Worcester. The modern A44 links this delightful little village readily to the busy centres of Moreton-in-Marsh and Broadway.

As with many small village churches, St Lawrence holds a treasure of the past safely within its ancient walls. Architectural features of 900 years are to be traced in its pillars and carving, its glass and font, its plate and monuments. The Winchester Bushel and Peck, made of bell metal and inscribed with the name of the Magistrate's Clerk, is of special interest. Dating from the time of Elizabeth I the weights and measures of the Winchester Standard – of such accuracy that they set the standard for the whole kingdom – were used to settle disputes relating to the collection of corn tithes.

One of the Cotswolds' finest and largest barns belongs to Bourton House at the east end at the foot of the hill.

▲ Once a humble farming village, Bourton bustles with visitors.

BOURTON-ON-THE-WATER

MAP REF: 90SP1620

Bourton-on-the-Water caters for visitors on a grand scale. Housed in an old watermill is a motor museum with one of the country's largest collections of vintage advertising signs. Exotic butterflies and model railways are on permanent exhibition in the High Street and perfume is made in the village.

So long established now as to form part of the village fabric are the Model Village and Birdland, both created by local men with great skill, both acclaimed the best of their kind in the world. The model, an exact replica of the village scaled down to one ninth the size of the original, is built of Cotswold stone in the garden of the Old New Inn.

Birdland, created by the late Len Hill – who was accorded the title 'Penguin Millionaire' when he bought two of the Falkland Islands simply to conserve their population of some one million penguins – is set in some eight acres of gardens. Close to the large public car park, Birdland's new home in Rissington Road is still expanding to accommodate its ever increasing bird life. It is very much a family business, with the largest collection of penguins outside America; indeed the Hill family even look after the RAF Red Arrows aerobatic flying team's mascot, Flight-Lieutenant Cedric, a distinguished pelican, just one of over 600 different breeds in this garden of birds.

The river, enhanced by attractive low bridges, is the outstanding natural feature of the village, earning it the label 'the little Venice of the Cotswolds'.

There was a bridge at Bourton in Roman times – a stone plaque on Bourton Bridge shows the badge of the Second Legion who laid out the Foss Way, which crosses the Windrush in a lovely valley of farmland where villagers have settled since the Iron Age. It would be hard to imagine any settlement so perfectly in harmony with its environment as this Cotswold stone-built village of today. Within easy reach are a dozen quiet villages and the well-marked footpath route across the dip-slope wolds of the Oxfordshire Way.

Folly Farm, a mere two and a half miles away, is a leading conservation centre for rare domestic waterfowl and poultry within its 160 different breeds.

BREDON AND ITS HILL VILLAGES

MAP REF: 80SO9236

A ring of villages encircles Bredon Hill as pretty as flowers in a garland. Vale-thatched Cotswold stone, timber and brick line the village streets and mix happily in cottage gardens.

Bredon to the south beckons with a slender church spire to its mainly one-street village of black and white, warm red brick and honey-coloured stone, a church with Norman work, mellowed houses of Elizabeth I's day, one of the largest tithe barns in England, and two of its oldest inns.

The low-lying river floods the Ham meadows in winter conserving the natural habitat for its flora and fauna, which together with the old village characters are immortalised in John Moore's *Brensham Village*, his name for Bredon.

The pretty hamlet of Bredon's Norton sheltering under the hill faces the Avon and the distant Malverns. 'Oh, pastoral heart of England' wrote Sir Arthur Quiller-Couch of Eckington Bridge. Despite its narrow width and long years the bridge has stood the test

▼ Bredon Church, its spire a landmark of this Cotswold vale village.

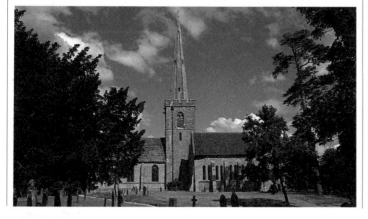

of time and 20th-century transport. Eckington is fruit-and-veg country, the coming of the Gloucester-to-Birmingham railway bringing its markets nearer in the mid-19th century.

The Combertons, Great and Little, pretty in all seasons, are a delight in apple-blossom time.

Two miles away arcing round the hill is Elmley Castle, a picture of black-and-white buildings brought alive by the singing of children dancing round the maypole on Oak Apple Day (29th May). The escape of the fugitive Charles I is kept fresh in the speech of local folk who call the way out of the village 'the hole in the wall'. This leads to Kersoe and on to Ashton-under-Hill, where farms abutting the streets once provided the living for the village.

There is still peace at Grafton' such as John Drinkwater knew. No new building since Victoria's day spoils the village of which the poet wrote, gathering folk songs in Beckford Inn and inspiration from the countryside.

The circle is completed through pretty little Conderton, visited by Joseph Arch to promote his Agricultural Workers' Union; along to parkland Overbury, visited by

THE COTSWOLD VOLUNTARY WARDEN SERVICE

The Cotswold Voluntary Warden Service was set up in 1968, two years after 582 square miles of the Cotswolds were designated an Area of Outstanding Natural Beauty. Today there is one full-time warden who is responsible for the work carried out by over 200 voluntary wardens, of all ages, recruited from all walks of life, who give their time and services free.

The wardens are always ready to help visitors with guidance and information when they meet on their regular patrols of footpaths, country parks and picnic sites. You will recognise them by their green and yellow armband or badge. They organise a regular series of guided walks including a number of specialised village walks. For the visitor who wishes to walk at his own speed they prepare and publish a series of walks leaflets (list and guided walks programmes available from the address below).

Wardens help to make walking in the Cotswolds even more enjoyable by regular patrols of the more popular footpaths (with the Cotswold Way as number one priority) to pin-point problems at an early stage. They then organise work parties to sort out difficulties by clearance work, by waymarking, or by building a stile or set of steps.

With the agreement and co-operation of landowners, wardens help to increase the beauty of areas to which the public have access by planting trees, by laying hedges, and by renewing and maintaining significant drystone walls. They occasionally clear scrubland in order to maintain an important wildlife habitat.

Wardens don't enjoy having to clear up litter which thoughtless people have left behind or deliberately dumped, but they do it! They will carry out litter clearance at a popular site to nip the problem in the bud before a major eyesore develops.

There are a number of experienced wardens who are willing to give illustrated talks about the Cotswolds and the Warden Service and who are trained to show related audio-visual programmes.

Wardens will help young people on the Duke of Edinburgh's Award Scheme by training them and involving them in practical work.

If you would like to know more about the Voluntary Warden Service or feel they might be able to help you in some way, write to:

Cotswold Warden Office,
c/o County Planning Department,
Gloucestershire County Council,
Shire Hall,
Gloucester GL1 2TN
or telephone:
Gloucester (0452) 425674.

▼ Voluntary wardens constructing a footbridge near Painswick.

▲ Much-visited beautiful Broadway.

John Wesley for overnight stabling for his horse and a bed for himself at the Court; and so to the long village of Kemerton. The latter can boast at least two famous residents: the 18th-century squire who built Parson's Folly on top of the hill to make it an even more prominent landmark, and the 20th-century writer, John Moore, who left the literary world the richer through his books about the hill villages of Bredon.

▼ Bredon Tithe Barn, showing its hand-railed tallet steps.

BROADWAY
MAP REF: 83SP0937

William Morris is said to have discovered Broadway and it is easy to see how he was captivated by this village of corn-coloured stone lying just off the scarpline on the rich soil of Worcestershire.

As English as apple pie, Broadway has remained as unchanged as is possible under the pressures of tourism, for it is a virtual honey-pot of visitors, and the village caters for them accordingly.

A bevy of artists followed in the wake of William Morris – his friend, Frank Millet, lived at Farnham House and died in the great Titanic disaster; J M Barrie, Vaughan Williams and Elgar – all drew inspiration from the line and form, texture and composition of what was then the typical English village.

The oldest of its two churches lies about a mile to the south of the village centre, on the Snowshill road. St Eadburgh's had served the villagers for seven centuries before the Victorians decided it was too much of a trek and built St Michael's close to the village green.

Arctophiles (teddy-bear collectors) are now beating a path to Broadway to the only Teddy Bear Museum in the Cotswolds, and one of the rare few in the country. Here, at the rear of the shop selling dolls and bears, is a collection of over 400 bears, including the earliest known teddy made by Margarete Steiff in 1903, and – yes – A A Milne's toy bear, on which he based the famous Winnie the Pooh!

The 'broad way' is the main street, lined with red chestnut trees. Situated on the main route between Oxford and Worcester, the village developed because of the stagecoach trade. Both King Charles and Oliver Cromwell stayed here at different times.

Of the many beautiful buildings it is the Lygon Arms (pronounced 'Liggon') that is the most striking. The success of the village as a staging-post really stems from the business acumen of General Lygon's butler who foresaw great potential in what was then the White Hart Inn. The butler bought the inn from his master and named it the Lygon Arms. Some two dozen inns opened up around the same time, and Broadway prospered since fresh and extra horses were in demand for the steep haul up the long Fish Hill on the A44 leading out of the village.

Fish Hill picnic site on the north side of the inn is a free area of 12 acres of grass and woodland with a nature trail, open all the year. A topograph puts names to the superb views; it is probably the only self-draining topograph in the country – for rain falling on the deeply incised Severn flows away! Over the road is the Broadway Tower Country Park.

▼ A floral welcome to a local pub.

BROADWAY TOWER COUNTRY PARK

MAP REF: 83SP1136

Almost as a punctuation mark on the north-westerly tip of the Cotswold escarpment, stands the Norman-style, battlemented dark tower on Broadway Beacon.

James Wyatt designed Broadway Tower in the late 18th century for the Sixth Earl of Coventry. He followed the fashion for follies as part of the landscaping of the estate by Capability Brown, yet chose a darker stone than the native Cotswold in order to create an appearance of brooding maturity.

At 1,024ft, the second highest point on the Cotswolds, the 65ft tower dominates the skyline above the village of Broadway and commands a panoramic view over a dozen counties; the keen-sighted can identify the distinctive lines of Warwick Castle, Worcester Cathedral and Tewkesbury Abbey.

◀ Ancient hostelries punctuate Burford's steep main street, descending down to the Windrush.

A telescope on the roof extends the range of vision on a clear day and a relief map on the third floor puts the landmarks into perspective.

William Morris, a frequent visitor, who wrote a letter from the Tower in 1876 which spearheaded the formation of the Society for the Protection of Ancient Buildings, is duly accorded a permanent exhibition on the second floor, and the eccentric bibliophile, Sir Thomas Phillips, who set up the Middle Hill Press in the Tower, is remembered by a printing press on the ground floor which visitors can use to print their own souvenirs.

Education and recreation happily merge: the Tower Barn is a typical Cotswold stone-built and tiled barn some 150 years old; a small model illustrates the age-old craft of Cotswold stone *slatting*, demonstrating how some 18,000 slates were used to roof the barn. A children's farmyard leads off the Country Classrooms. An adventure playground, containing England's only whirligig, ball games, barbecue and picnic areas, animal enclosures, and refreshments in Rookery Barn with its terrace overlooking giant chess and draughts games ensure plenty to occupy the family.

Nature walks lead through woodland and to the Fish Inn on the busy A44, and follow, albeit briefly, the road where Roman legions once marched across the Cotswolds.

BURFORD

MAP REF: 91SP2512

This is the stone country of the Cotswolds; from the quarries on the eastern edge came the easily worked oolite limestone to rebuild many of London's churches after the Great Fire, St Paul's Cathedral, Blenheim Palace, Oxford's colleges and the Sheldonian Theatre – and Burford.

Burford's long main street descends steeply down the hill in Lilliputian scale against a backcloth of softly moulded wold and water-meadow. Grey-gabled houses with lichen-encrusted roofs, shops and tearooms, haughty-height hotels and comforting old inns line the street; a jumbled juxtaposition of home and trading post, resident and tourist sleeping together under a roof ridge crookedly sloped against the skyline. A line of limes in a wide grass verge separates the buildings from the road down to the memorial cross.

The Tolsey, a market house of Tudor date, now housing the museum, holds out its great round clock as though to remind visitors to take time to explore the by-streets and back-lanes of this old grey town. The ancient Priory, now a closed nunnery, lies to the west, holding the memories of 'pretty witty Nell' and her merry monarch within its austere walls. Their son born in 1670 was created Earl of Burford and Nell Gwyn named her rooms at Windsor Burford House.

It was the famous races across the seven downs to the south-west that brought royalty and riff-raff, gentlefolk and gamblers to cram the town. This great sporting event, that lasted over 200 years,

▼ A panoramic patchwork of Vale Country and wide blue hills between Warwick and the Black mountains, as seen from Broadway Tower roof.

declined with the enclosure of the open fields, but the new coaching era boosted the town economy and left fine old hostelries in its wake.

The church with its splendid spire stands to the east at the foot of the hill in a pocket of history. A Royalist captive left the word 'prisner' and the date scratched inside the font; Warwick 'the Kingmaker' left a legacy of fine old almshouses, and Symon Wysdom, an alderman, founded the first school here in 1577.

The northerly point of the town terminates at the low stone bridge; across the river is countryside. On the high road to the south is the Cotswold Wildlife Park, where animals from all over the world roam in 200 acres of beautiful gardens and woodland.

CHEDWORTH
MAP REF: 88SP0511

Settled amid a patchwork of fields is Chedworth – its stone-built cottages scattered among pretty gardens on the steep hillsides bounding the Coln valley.

Fine old cottages of the mid-18th century radiate from a church with Norman foundations and a manor house with medieval origins, grouped on the typical English village plan. Steep-pitched gables and mullioned windows typify the Cotswold style in large and small houses alike, and the visit of Elizabeth of York 500 years ago is perpetuated in Queen Street.

Above the village at Denfurlong a farm trail is open all the year allowing an insight into modern dairy and arable farming.

Sheltered in a beautiful combe, Chedworth Roman Villa is the best exposed Romano-British villa in Britain. Built in about AD 120, it was occupied until about AD 400. The mosaic floors in the bath suites and triclinium are fine examples of the craft practised some 1500 years ago. Particularly beautiful is the one in the west wing where figures depicting the four seasons are shown in each corner. Fascinating finds and plans of the site are displayed in the adjacent museum which, together with the villa, is owned by the National Trust.

CHELTENHAM SPA
MAP REF: 87SO9422

'Pretty, poor and proud' – Cheltenham has attracted more elegant titles over the years, but a local maxim is always worth looking at in detail.

Cheltenham spreads along a terrace under the great bluff of Cleeve Hill, the highest point of the Cotswolds and above the flat vale lands watered by the Severn.

It is pretty. The Promenade has been described as the most beautiful thoroughfare in Britain. It is outstanding in its composition of elegant Regency buildings separated from the main road by wide flower-bedded greens and an avenue of some of the town's estimated 80,000 trees. High-class shops and boutiques making a bustling contrast on the opposite side.

There is no evidence of poverty in Cheltenham today – rather it is smart, fashionable and prosperous. It is generally regarded as the western gateway to the Cotswolds.

▲ Regency elegance in opulent Cheltenham Spa.

Prestigious festivals of music and literature attract lovers of the arts to star-studded programmes and royalty attend the races at nearby Prestbury. Gustav Holst was born at Number 4 Clarence Road in 1874 and his Regency birthplace with Victorian furnishings is open to the public. The Art Gallery and Museum houses the internationally famous Arts and Crafts Movement collection, and the Pittville Pump Room Museum boasts Britain's most complete Regency room.

Proud, it certainly is. Cheltenham succeeded where others in the area failed. From its humble beginnings as a moderate little market town in constant competition with neighbouring Prestbury – each inhibiting the growth of the other – Cheltenham was virtually just a single street in 1779, even though it did stretch for almost a mile.

Within 20 years its population had quadrupled; within the 150 years it had attracted some 60,000 more inhabitants.

To the three p's should be added a fourth – for pigeons – for the success story of Cheltenham began with pigeons. In what was, in 1716, a meadow outside the little town (and is now the Ladies' College) a number of pigeons were found to be pecking at what turned out to be salt crystals at a spring. The owner railed in the spot, raised a thatched shed over it and gave Cheltenham its first pump-room. Henry Skillicorne, his astute son-in-law, built a more permanent and presentable edifice to house the spring in 1748, improved the approach to it and called it a spa.

Physicians wrote long treatises on the medicinal virtues of the waters, and George III stamped them with the royal seal of approval by 'taking them' in a five-week holiday at Cheltenham in 1788. The shortage of the waters soon afterwards seemed like the demise which the old radical, William Cobbett, had hoped for. He saw the town as a sink for plunderers and drunkards and debauchees of all descriptions. Others saw it as 'the favourite resort of fashion and the shrine of health'. Jane Austen stayed for three weeks in 1816 and wrote 'How much is Cheltenham to be preferred in May'; she was obviously there to 'take the waters' as in the same letter to her sister Cassandra, she reveals that 'the Duchess of Orléans drinks at my pump'. New wells were sunk, the spa water flowed and visitors arrived by the trainload. The town put the pigeons in its coat of arms.

41

▲ Sunlight captured on Cotswold stone in a Chipping Campden street.

CHIPPING CAMPDEN

MAP REF: 83SP1539

On Campden wold the skylark
* sings,*
In Campden town the traveller
* finds*
The inward peace that beauty
* brings*
To bless and heal tormented
* minds.*

John Masefield certainly captured the essence of Chipping Campden, in the north Cotswolds, the most beautiful of all the market towns,

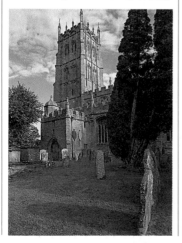

for it wears its age with serenity and compels the visitor to slow down and take stock of its charm.

History in stone is the town's motto. Stone of honey-gold deepening to tawny-brown built the houses, shops, inns, tea-rooms and hotels standing shoulder to shoulder lining both sides of the long High Street. Steeply-pitched roofs, bold chimneys, gables and mullions, dormers and sundials and deep-set doorways pointed with shadow give them individual character.

The Church of St James stands at the westerly edge of the town; with its impressive pinnacled tower it is one of the most splendid of the Cotswold wool churches and is a veritable treasure-house of the town's past. The largest memorial brass in Gloucestershire is here – to William Grevel 'the flower of the wool merchants of all England'.

Church Street is a pocket of history. Close to the church are the Jacobean lodges and gateway – all that remains of the old manor of Campden. On the raised pavement is a row of almshouses

◀ The great Perpendicular church with its 13th-century doorway.

built in the reign of King James I in stunning symmetry. The walled dip opposite is an old cartwheel wash.

On entering the High Street, Grevel House is on the right. Built in the 14th century it is distinguished by a Perpendicular bay window. Woolstaplers Hall on the left is a near contemporary and is now the town museum and tourist information centre.

The gabled Market Hall was built by Sir Baptist Hicks in 1627 to provide shelter for the stalls selling butter, cheese and poultry. The memorial cross and ancient town hall share its island in the middle of the High Street.

▼ Simplicity of style in full splendour at Chipping Campden.

In Sheep Street is the old silk mill where C R Ashbee centred his Guild of Handicrafts – the Hart family of silversmiths continue the tradition today.

Tradition is strong in Chipping Campden. Its outstanding architecture is preserved by the Campden Trust, formed in 1929, which also fosters the craft movement. A separate society re-established the ancient Dover Games which take place on the hill above the town each Spring Bank Holiday, and followed the next day by a colourful street carnival called the Scuttlebrook Wake.

CHIPPING NORTON

MAP REF: 85SP3127

Norton gained its Chipping, the medieval term for market, in the time of King John and evolved as a typical wool town with the traditional Perpendicular-style church as witness to its piety and prosperity. The rough justice of Henry VIII's day put the church to impious use when the town's vicar was hanged from the steeple for refusing to use Cranmer's English prayer book. St Mary's with its unusual hexagonal porch, has many fine features.

Chipping Norton's most notable landmark is the tall chimney stack of Bliss Tweed Mill, an impressive Victorian building of an earlier mill producing tweeds outstanding for their durability.

There is much in this little town that endures its changing economy: a row of gabled almshouses in Cotswold stone, Market Street and Middle Row where old buildings adapt to modern-day trading, and a splendid little theatre in Spring Street.

CIRENCESTER
MAP REF: 93SP0201

The Romans called it Corinium; gentlefolk and country folk alike stick to Shakespeare's 'Cicester'; the indifferent say 'Siren'.

Only London was larger than Roman Corinium, which grew up at the intersection of the three major roads – the Foss Way, Ermin Way and Akeman Street.

Its strategic position on such a vital road junction and its sophistication did not impress the Saxons, who preferred to build smaller settlements outside the town walls, except for their church which was the longest parish church in England.

Cirencester regained its status under Norman rule for they realised the potential of its central position on the major trading routes, and it became the most important town in the Cotswolds for the medieval wool trade.

The pivot of modern Cirencester is the parish church – the largest in Gloucestershire and a splendid monument to the stonemasons' skills in an age when wealth and good taste went together. For all its splendour, it is the magnificent south porch which is the outstanding feature. Built by the abbots at the end of the 15th century as an office, it became the Town Hall after the Dissolution.

Cirencester parish church can also boast the oldest peal of 12 bells in England. And the tower observes some of the more ancient of campanological customs, including the ringing of the 'Pancake Bell' on Shrove Tuesday and the celebration of the Restoration at dawn on 29 May.

As with other towns, building and rebuilding has altered the overall complexion, but at ground level there is much charm to this country town. Stall-holders with their clutter and clamour fill the centre market-place; ancient hostelries range from horse brass-decked bars to Continental-style courtyards. Becoming rarer, and therefore more precious to the character of Cirencester, are the old established family butchers and bakers, coffee shops and ironmongers, florists and fishmongers and high-class jewellers, although a younger generation of craftsmen keeps old skills alive in a converted brewery.

The Corinium Museum in Park Street is renowned for its important Roman collection, including mosaics.

Ancient buildings are preserved in such splendid examples as the Weavers Hall, the arches of St John's Hospital, Spitalgate, St Laurence's Almshouses and Coxwell Street. The only monastic survival is the Norman gatehouse in Grove Lane.

The old Corn Hall, housing the Information Centre in the Market Place, is the forum for regular craft and antique markets. The town's agricultural past has given Cirencester its Mop Fairs in September and along with the town carnival still attract crowds in their season to this ancient market town.

The Abbey grounds are a delight, with swans on the Churn, the monks' gnarled old mulberry tree propped up alongside the path and acres of grass for the public to enjoy.

Cirencester Park, the seat of Lord Bathurst, is also open to the public, but the mansion, behind one of the largest yew hedges in the world, is not. The park is the finest surviving example in England of geometrical landscaping where great rides meet and grand vistas disappear into decreasing distances. Polo, the game of royal princes, is regularly played at Cirencester Park.

▼ Coxwell Street, a part of Cirencester hardly altered in 300 years.

CLEEVE HILL

MAP REF: 81SO9826

The B4632 looping south-westwards from Winchcombe to Cheltenham follows the contour of Cleeve Hill as it juts its massive bulk out of the westerly escarpment.

Following the undulating course due south along the escarpment gives excellent views over the Vale of Gloucester with the famous Prestbury racecourse on the northern periphery of Cheltenham below. The summit at 1,083ft is at the head of West Down at the southern point of the Common.

Cleeve Common on the high plateau is the gallops on which such famous jockeys as Fred Archer and Black Tom Oliver trained. Along with Happy Valley, further south, Cleeve Common covers an area of some 3 square miles. It is a Site of Special Scientific Interest, scheduled as Grade I on account of its natural beauty.

Butterflies can be sent up in clouds on a good day; musk, frog and bee orchids are among the rarer of the wild flowers with the delicate harebell and hardy gorse providing strong contrasts.

Sheltering in an almost hidden valley below the north-easterly edge of the Common is the enchanting grouping of Jacobean manor-house, Tudor tithe barn and what is thought to be the oldest Roman Catholic chapel in the county. Postlip Hall, set in acres of unspoilt grounds, is sometimes open to the public. Higher up the valley and closer to the main road is Postlip Mill, the only surviving papermaking mill in the county.

THE COTSWOLDS AND THEIR GOLDEN FLEECE

'In Europe the best wool is English; in England the best wool is Cotswold.' So ran the saying in Norman England, but the Cotswolds were exporting *fells* (the whole sheepskin on the hide of slaughtered animals) as early as AD 700 to English missionaries abroad.

Under Norman rule the export of wool increased considerably to meet the demands of the prestigious cloth industry of the Flemish weavers. Norman knights were rewarded for their services in the Conquest with vast estates, and they and the large numbers of monastic foundations increased their revenue by increasing their sheep-holdings. In the 20 years following the great Domesday census the sheep population outnumbered the people by four to one.

The Cotswold, the ancient breed descended from the Roman longwool sheep, thrived on the limestone-rich herbage to become the largest sheep in England. Named after the Cotswold hills (*cot* being a biblical term for enclosing sheep, and *wold* meaning rolling hillside) they grew long and heavy fleeces with strong curl and rich lustre. By the Middle Ages the whole Cotswold countryside was one vast sheepwalk.

THE COTSWOLD BREED

▲ Cotswold 'Lion' ewe with lambs, so named for its 'mane' of wool.

Wealthy wool merchants rebuilt the old churches in Perpendicular style and enriched them with fine carvings and glorious stained glass windows. The finest examples of these wool churches are at Chipping Campden, Northleach, Cirencester, Fairford and Lechlade, where memorial brasses give some indication of the likeness of the old woolmen and their wives.

Wool became the most powerful political weapon. The wool merchants became creditors to the aristocracy and kings drew large incomes from the wool tax. The Chancellor was so delighted with the wool whose revenue accounted for over half of England's total wealth that he plumped himself down on a sack

▼ Cleeve Hill is well-walked on the westward scarp line. (Inset) AA topograph on Frocester Hill.

of Cotswold wool in Parliament. The Chancellor's seat is still a woolsack.

Eventually the taxes which raised the revenue crippled the wool trade. Cloth-making took over from sheep-farming and centred in the Stroud valleys where the abundant springs and strong water supply powered the mills. It was then the turn of the rich clothiers, who built fine houses for themselves in Cotswold style and of local stone, further enriching the architectural scene with domestic buildings.

The Industrial Revolution started the collapse, the introduction of synthetic fibres and the increased importation of cheaper cloths accelerated the decline of the once famous Cotswold woollen industry.

However, all is not history. Quality cloth is still produced in a couple of mills in the Stroud valley and across the Cotswolds in a converted stone barn at Filkins. The Cotswold Woollen Weavers card and spin and weave from the fleece, and visitors can see the processes for themselves amid the clack of shuttles, the rumble of looms and the evocative smells of machine oil and raw wool. And in small flocks on the rolling hill country can still be seen the Cotswolds, now a protected rare breed kept by keen members of the Cotswold Sheep Society.

▲ Cottage-style manor house at Cold Aston in the Cotswold uplands.

COALEY PEAK AND FROCESTER HILL PICNIC SITE

MAP REF: 78SO7901

Some 3 miles south-west of Stroud, on the B4066, Coaley Peak picnic site makes a fine point from which to explore the surrounding countryside as it is open all the year. Jointly owned and managed by the County Council and the National Trust, there is an information centre with display boards, illustrating the locality and its wildlife. Books are available on walks in the area.

Coaley Peak is typical of the limestone grassland to be found on the Cotswold scarp edge grazed in the summer months by a small flock of the ancient breed of Cotswold sheep. Within a short walking distance on Frocester Hill is Nympsfield Long Barrow. Named by the Celts as 'Shrine Field', the barrow is an interesting example of the early true-entrance Severn-Cotswold type and was excavated in 1937. Hetty Pegler's Tump, a short distance away, is a chambered long barrow with access by a key held at Crawley Barns.

Coaley lies about a mile off; Frocester down its steep hill is a delightful vale village with a pretty gatehouse to its old Court. Frocester tithe barn is enormous, remarkable in both its construction and preservation for it dates back to around 1300.

An AA topograph on Frocester Hill identifies points of interest in the extensive views over the Severn Vale, Forest of Dean and the hills of Wales in the distance.

COLD ASHTON

MAP REF: 78ST7472

The most southerly of the Cotswold hill villages, Cold Ashton, exposed to the prevailing sou'westerlies which blow straight off the Bristol Channel, is aptly named; but high up on the plateau above Bath the early medieval farmers established a vineyard on the south-facing slopes, and farms have grown round it ever since.

The church is perhaps more remarkable for having been largely rebuilt in Tudor times at the personal expense of the rector, rather than for any notable architectural merit. The Revd Thomas Key 'signed' his work both at the doorway and on a chantry window with the letter T entwined in a key. The oak pulpit has an exquisite stone canopy, quite rare in a Cotswold church and uncommonly beautiful.

It is the manor-house which attracts all the attention: Cold Ashton Manor has been described as the most perfect example of an Elizabethan house in all England. It is, unfortunately, not open to the public. From here, down the lovely St Catherine's Valley, the Limestone Link, a newly-opened footpath route, extends the Cotswold Way by 40 miles, winding through the hills beyond Bath to join the West Mendip Way.

COLD ASTON

MAP REF: 90SP1219

Cold Aston is often confused linguistically with Cold Ashton in the south Cotswolds, but apart from their exposed upland position (both stand at 700 feet above sea level) they have nothing else in common. Cold Aston has laboured under two names for over 400 years – and still does as can be seen on the signposts to and in the village.

Domesday is specific: *Eston* (Aston). Episcopal records are the first to qualify it as *frigida* in 1287, and it remained as such, or sometimes *cold*, until 1554 when a Patent Roll announced the appointment of a vicar to *Aston Blank*. The right of presentation by then had passed to the Crown so for what reason the name was foisted on the village remains a mystery.

Aston Blank it became to church, education and postal authorities and the Inland Revenue. The inhabitants stoically stuck to Cold Aston, as did those who embroidered the church banners. The Ordnance Survey alternated the names on successive maps; the Highways Division plays safe and uses the alias.

Of paramount importance is the fact that it is a complete village; it has a shop and a school – rare facilities in small places today. On the tiny green stands a huge sycamore tree – one of the largest and oldest in England. The Norman church has no east window; a rare unaltered feature of early Celtic origin to be found in only four other Cotswold churches – Notgrove, Baunton, Winston and Brimpsfield. And, in the attractive 17th-century Plough Inn the question will still be asked: is this Cold Aston or Aston Blank?

THE COLNS

MAP REF: 94SP0810 and 95SP1405

The Coln, winding its way from the small Clevely brook off the high easterly slopes of Cleeve Hill to meet the Thames at Lechlade, runs through the heart of the Cotswolds. Three valley villages take their names from the river.

Coln St Dennis, the most northerly, is reached off the old Roman Foss Way, now the A429, at Fossebridge. A pocket-sized place of breath-taking simplicity, it is a honey-coloured Cotswold stone cluster of manor and farm, cottages and church. It takes its name from the church of St Dionisius of Paris to whom its lands were granted by William the Conqueror. The Norman church, with its modest squat tower, is dedicated to St James and stands in a tranquil spot on the riverside.

Coln Rogers, downstream, has work of even older hands to show, for its church retains a Saxon nave and chancel and quoining of its large stones in the long-and-short style. Originally known as Coln St Andrews, from the church dedication, the small village assumed the name Rogers from its patron, Roger de Gloucester, when he presented its living to that Abbey around 1100. West of the church an arched doorway to a shed-like ruin is possibly the remains of a 14th-century priest's house.

Coln St Aldwyns, separated from its upstream sisters by some six miles and the lovely village of Bibury, has the same charm but on a larger scale. This time it was the patron saint of the church which was changed. Formerly dedicated to the hermit saint, Ealdwine, the church favoured St John the Baptist in the 13th century.

▲ Snug thatch in the Coln valley.

The village radiates in four directions. Sturdy stone cottages set back in pretty gardens line the main street running north to south, with the gardens hiding to the rear as the cottages descend the hill to the old mill at the bottom. A magnificent chestnut tree stands sentinel as the east–west road crosses over at the top of the hill.

A cul-de-sac of manorial farm, barns and cottages groups with the church to the west; to the east is Williamstrip Park, the classical 17th-century mansion built in a commanding position over rolling parkland.

At Quenington, a mile away, the tiny church has beautiful Romanesque doorways; the first known in Europe, after Reading Abbey, to portray the Coronation of the Virgin.

COOPER'S HILL LOCAL NATURE RESERVE

MAP REF: 86SO8914

Cooper's Hill, owned by the County Council, is a massive spur of the west scarp edge about five miles south-east of Gloucester. The nature reserve of about 137 acres is within a larger area scheduled by English Nature as a Site of Special Scientific Interest.

Its strategic position giving extensive views over the vale was realised as early as 500 BC when local tribes made it what was then one of the largest Iron Age encampments in the county.

Roman soldiers passed this way and, according to local tradition, left their ghosts behind them. A spring on the east side of the hill and a villa at nearby Witcombe are more settled and tangible evidence of their occupation.

A superb nature trail, passing through lovely woodland of beech, birch, sycamore and ash, and over open grassland to take in the vale views, is easily approached from Fiddler's Elbow on the A46, where there is space for parking.

The apex of the trail is the maypole on the northern tip, marking the point from where the Whitsuntide cheese-rolling race starts. The festival was once a hilarious mix of rustic revelry.

The programme of 1836 included dancing for the ribbons worn by the Master of Ceremonies, *shimey to be ron for* (girls raced for the prize of a chemise), and *a bladder of snuff to be chatred for by hold wimming* (the old woman who chattered the longest and loudest won the snuff). The races down (and one up) the hill are still included today in a much more decorous, but still colourful, custom.

CRANHAM

MAP REF: 86SO8912

The village settles in a deep hollow of ancient beech woods, named by the Saxons. Where they reach out to the high escarpment near Birdlip they hide the source from which the River Frome springs.

The Church of St James overlooks the village. Two pairs of sheep-shears are carved on the tower, symbols of the wool trade whose merchants built the church. Hands of all centuries have furnished it but it was the Victorians who enlarged it.

Cranham is one of the beauty spots of the Cotswolds and its annual Feast and Ox Roast is a typical village affair attracting visitors from far and wide each August.

▼ Evening sun at Coln St Aldwyns.

RALPH VAUGHAN WILLIAMS

Down Ampney appears above the hymn 'Come down, O Love Divine' in the Church of England's English Hymnal 1906. It is the title of the music composed by Dr Ralph Vaughan Williams and commemorates his birthplace in the south-eastern corner of the Cotswolds.

Born on 12th October 1872 at the Old Vicarage – which was then only seven years old – Ralph Vaughan Williams was the youngest of three children of the vicar, Arthur Charles Vaughan Williams and his wife Margaret, daughter of Josiah Wedgwood III.

He was only three years old when his father died and his mother returned to the family home in Surrey where the children were brought up. A stained glass window was inserted in the old stone Church of All Saints in memory of the young vicar, who is buried close to the south porch in the quiet churchyard touching the wood-edged fields at one end of the village of Down Ampney.

Initially educated at home, Vaughan Williams went to preparatory school, where he showed an early aptitude for the violin and pianoforte. At Charterhouse he progressed to the viola and organ and entered the Royal College of Music in 1890. Later, while at Trinity College, Cambridge, he continued his weekly lessons with Sir Hubert Parry. In 1908 he studied with Ravel in Paris.

▲ Ralph Vaughan Williams honoured his Cotswold home in a hymn.

During the years 1902–12 Dr Vaughan Williams collected traditional folk-songs, writing the words and notes of the tune as the singer sang in the harvest field, or in a cottage or the local inn – a laborious task which he obviously undertook in the light of what he said had been inculcated in him by his old teacher, Max Bruch, 'you must not write eye music; you must write ear music'.

His symphonies and folk-songs alike were in characteristically English style, earning him the respect and admiration of music-lovers everywhere and the Order of Merit from George V.

Although fate and fame kept him in London, Vaughan Williams was frequently in the Cotswolds; he followed William Morris at Broadway, and the ancient drove roads, such as the Welsh Way, feature in his Cotswold opera *Hugh the Drover*. He composed for and conducted several times at the Three Choirs Festival at Gloucester, and just two years before his death attended a production at the Cheltenham College. Gustav Holst, his closest friend from their student days, was born at Cheltenham.

When Vaughan Williams died in 1958, he was buried in Westminster Abbey, and the music that accompanied the procession to the grave was the one which he had composed to honour his Cotswold birthplace – Down Ampney.

▲ Expansive vista of heaven and earth leads to Crickley Hill.

CRICKLEY HILL COUNTRY PARK

MAP REF: 86SO9316

Crickley Hill is a promontory of the escarpment. It overshadows the A417 as it leaves the Air Balloon public house on the corner to descend to Gloucester.

The hill-fort to the south-west of the park is the site of one of the most important archaeological discoveries in Europe. Over the last two decades some 3,500 volunteers from many countries have helped to excavate the site. Perhaps not as dramatic in its artefacts as some, but none the less interesting, the annual summer 'digs' here have revealed evidence of almost uninterrupted habitation from the Stone Age. Iron Age defences, a beaker from early Bronze Age, flint arrowheads, an ancient shrine and a military buckle from the 5th century BC all testify to the populace who would, as today's visitor can, marvel at the expansive view the hill site affords. On a clear day the Brecon Beacons, some 53 miles away, can be seen. An information centre close by the car park and a site warden in the summer months ensure the visitor can interpret the many facets of the country park.

DAGLINGWORTH AND THE DUNTISBOURNES

MAP REF: 93SO9708 to 93SO9905

The Saxons came off the Roman Ermin Way (A417) to this sequestered valley three miles north-east of Cirencester, and, at Daglingworth, much of their stonemasons' skill remains – in a sundial over the church doorway and a Crucifixion scene on the exterior of the chancel. Holy Rood Church stands on a bank above the village, which clusters in groups, like gossips, on both sides of the stream. The manor forms its own nucleus at Lower End, with a circular medieval dovecote among the traditional angles of houses large and small.

The Duntisbournes nestle in knots upstream. Tucked into the fold of the wooded hill valley, they take their name from the Duntisbourne brook which knits them together with Daglingworth before it joins the Churn.

Duntisbourne Rouse is an idyllic spot caught in a hollow of green hills, with a ford in the bottom and a saddleback-towered church on a steep bank.

Middle Duntisbourne, settled around another ford, is a farming hamlet of Duntisbourne Leer, itself a hamlet of Duntisbourne Abbots.

Fleurs-de-lys carved on chimney and doorhead of a farmhouse and the Leer in its name echo the manor's early ownership by the Abbey of Lire in Normandy.

Duntisbourne Abbots, possessed by St Peter's Abbey of Gloucester, perpetuates those early ties in the names of the village and dedication of its church. Unusual centre-pivoted gates make true use of the lych-gate.

DOWN AMPNEY
MAP REF: 94SU1097

Separated from the other three Ampney villages by some 4 miles of flat meadowlands, Down Ampney has an almost suburban appearance with its house-lined long street.

At the very end of the village, in a peaceful tree-shaded corner, is the medieval Down Ampney House, its Tudor gatehouse seen now only in old engravings. All Saints Church is a venerable neighbour, furnished with the work of many centuries.

Down Ampney is a place of pilgrimage to honour its past heroes. Sir Nicholas Villiers is shown in coat-of-mail, as befits a Crusader. Today's Knights Hospitallers return each year adding a touch of pageantry to this quiet spot.

World War II airmen are commemorated in a stained-glass window in the church, a plaque at the end of the runway from which they flew and an annual service; and music lovers pause reverently at the gate of the Old Vicarage – the birthplace of Vaughan Williams.

▼ Thirteenth-century All Saints' Church.

DURSLEY
MAP REF: 78ST7597

Dursley's early manorial ties with the powerful Berkeleys, who held the long-lost castle there, were severed as the town turned from its feudal masters to seek new prosperity in the woollen industry.

Depressed but by no means defeated by the decline in woollen manufacture, the mill owners put their industrial expertise into new enterprises. Engineering development from metalsmiths and Listers of Dursley, who first came to the town to serve the weaving mills, must be the success story of the century, producing everything from diesel engines to sheep-shears.

The 15th-century Church of St James, built of local tufa, had its tower rebuilt in 1707–1709 after the collapse of the original tower and spire.

Streets with the history of the town wrapped up in their names branch out from the central Market Place. The Market House has a bell in its turret and Queen Anne in a niche holding centre-stage. A literary circle to the east of the town at Whiteway comprises roads dedicated to Wordsworth, Byron, Kipling, Tennyson and Chaucer, with Shakespeare Road the longest, presumably on account of his short stay in the town in 1585 when he was sought by the Lord of the Manor not for his talents as a poet but as a poacher!

Roads leading westward out of the town rise steeply along the Broadway to Stinchcombe Hill, an 18-hole golf course and an area open to the public affording panoramic views.

The neighbouring village of Uley, famed for its blue broadcloth which has clothed generations of British military, was built mainly from the neolithic promontory fort at Uleybury half a mile away, one of the best examples in the country.

FAIRFORD
MAP REF: 95SP1500

'Faireforde never flourished afore ye Tames came to it', wrote Leland, antiquary to Henry VIII, of this Coln valley market town in the south-east corner of the Cotswolds.

It is to old John Tame's church, St Mary's, focal point of the main street, that visitors have been attracted for five centuries. The magnet is the only complete set of medieval stained glass windows to survive in the whole of the British Isles. Their design is now generally attributed to Barnard Flower, 'Master Glass Painter' to Henry VII. This is borne out by the fact that John Tame, a wealthy wool merchant, who rebuilt the church and endowed it with the magnificent windows, was a tenant of the Tudors and everywhere in the fine 'wool' church is to be seen the Tudor rose carving. It is to the windows that the eye is constantly drawn – locally and anciently they were known as 'the poor man's bible', depicting in glowing jewel-like colours the pictoral story of the entire Catholic faith.

South of the noble church is the former school, an endowment of three ladies of the manor, of which Elizabeth Farmor was the greatest benefactor and from whom the school took its name. Farmor's moved to new buildings in the park, on the site of the old manor-house, in 1961, and the substantial stone building is now the community centre. Contiguous to the old school is Fairford House, an elegant contemporary building on the site of the Tames' family house.

The Bull Hotel flanks the entire west side of the market-place, ending in a half-timbered building, formerly the George Inn.

The mainly 18th-century High Street reflects the prosperity of the age when Fairford was a major

posting town on the Gloucester to London coach run. Sandwiched between Park Street, with its medieval dovecote and cottages all in a row, prettily aproned with tiny gardens, and London Street on the A417 is the Croft with the county's smallest cottage hospital.

The Coln separates the ancient borough from the old 'milltown' west end – a rural expanse of meadow and mill – terminated by a mix of farm and residential area on the site of an ancient Saxon settlement.

FILKINS
MAP REF: 79SP2404

Cotswold Woollen Weavers is the sign that catches the eye of motorists speeding along the A361 between Burford and Lechlade. The sinuous route along which the packhorses and wool-laden waggons trundled over the centuries from the markets of Campden to the docks at Southampton has now been bypassed and the little village of Filkins cut off from arterial traffic.

Filkins is just over the county border in Oxfordshire. Its character is totally Cotswold, built from locally quarried stone. Stone is the outstanding feature of Filkins. The huge rectangular slabs fastened together with iron clamps came from the Long Ground Quarry; peculiar to Filkins, they edge the cottage gardens looking

▲ The Cotswold Woollen Weavers are the centrestone of a thriving craftwork complex at Filkins.

▲ Despite extensive rebuilding, St Michael's Church retains its original Norman doorways.

for all the world like thin and hoary headstones. One *slat*, for the slabs are really Cotswold stone tiles, completely roofs the old village lock-up, twinned cosily to the tiny cottage which houses the most incredible local collection to be found anywhere. Formed through the acquisitive acumen of the late George Swinford, and the philanthropic foresight of its greatest benefactor, Sir John Cripps, Filkins Museum was the model for the University of Reading's great Museum of Country Life.

The whole village concept is a model of how initiative and enterprise can be engineered into making rural areas thriving communities again. Craft

workshops have settled into disused farm buildings at the end of the village: rush weavers, a furniture restorer and a stonemason have already joined the woollen weavers, who spin, card and weave in a beautiful 18th-century Cotswold barn. In a nearby farmhouse, the Cotswold Dyers dye wools with natural plant materials.

GUITING POWER AND COTSWOLD FARM PARK

MAP REF: 89SP0924 and 83SP1126

The Guitings take their name from their position on the upper reaches of the Windrush in the north Cotswolds. *Gyte* is Old English for

'flood' and Power was the name of the local family. Guiting Power was originally called Nether Guiting from its siting lower down the valley from its twin, Temple Guiting – so distinguished by belonging to the Knights Templar.

Farms are dotted along the banks where the streams from Guiting Wood and the willow-lined valley meet, and sturdy cottages close in on the picturesque village green.

In the heart of quarry-land, Guiting Power has made good use of its stone in simple and traditional style, its attraction being that of grouping by purpose rather than for individual design.

Above the village, on the open rolling wolds is Bemborough Farm, the centre and shop window of the Rare Breeds Survival Trust. Cotswold Farm Park is an adjunct to the working farm and since its opening in 1970 has drawn families and students, conservationists, television, film crews and the press to see the ancient breeds of farm animals and fowl in a natural farm environment. Here you can see the Cotswold sheep, which once carried the wealth of medieval England on their backs, the Old Gloucester cows and the Gloucester Old Spot pigs.

Seaweed-eating Orkneys, oxen, cattle, boars, goats and every endangered species of British farm animal are of interest to the visitor and serve a serious purpose in the fight for survival. Educational facilities are an important feature of the Farm Park with seasonal attractions such as sheep-shearing and special exhibitions. A children's corner is a great favourite, where tiny tots can roam freely with tiny animals.

▲ Romantic ruins of Hailes Abbey echo of its original magnificence.

HAILES

MAP REF: 82SP0430

Hailes is a hauntingly beautiful ruin of an abbey once so magnetic that it drew royalty and pilgrims alike to this remote little spot.

Winchcombe was already a powerful monastic seat by the time of the Conquest, and when Ralph de Worcester fortified a small castle at Hailes and built a church in about 1130 the Abbot of Winchcombe clawed in a compensatory pension of seven shillings a year and exercised a considerable measure of dominance over the church. This simple building, no larger than a barn, has medieval paintings on the walls, heraldic tiles on the floor, and a tranquillity that only 800 years endow.

Winchcombe was no doubt more incensed but powerless to intervene when Hailes was chosen as the site for a new monastery for the Cistercian Order.

As a thanksgiving for having survived a shipwreck, Richard, Earl of Cornwall and King of the Romans, built the magnificent abbey on land granted for the purpose by his brother Henry III. Consecrated in 1251, Hailes attracted rich and poor, the noble, the infirm and the penitent after Edmund, Earl Richard's son, presented the abbey with a phial authenticated as containing the blood of Christ but later found to be false. The main buildings were destroyed in the Dissolution of the Monasteries in 1539.

Graceful arches and stony outlines of the ground plan are all that remain of the building, but in the adjacent museum there are many exhibits excavated from the site to indicate its former glory.

BEATRIX POTTER IN THE COTSWOLDS

'And the queerest thing about it is – I heard it in Gloucestershire, and it is true! at least the tailor, the waistcoat, and the "No more twist".'

The Tailor of Gloucester, which Beatrix Potter called 'my own favourite amongst the little books', was written as a Christmas present in 1901 for her little friend called Freda Moore.

It was while visiting her cousins, Judge Crompton Hutton and his family, at Harescombe Grange, near Stroud, that Beatrix Potter first heard the story 'from Miss Caroline Hutton, who had it of Miss Lucy of Gloucester, who had it of the tailor'.

The tailor who was the centre of the ladies' gossip at their tea-party was then a very young man, John Prichard of Gloucester, who had been commissioned to make a special waistcoat for the new mayor to wear in an important procession through the city.

The tailor was very busy and the great day was nearly upon him. On the Saturday he left his tailor's shop with the special waistcoat only just cut out. When he returned on the Monday he was astonished to find it finished – except for one buttonhole. A little note pinned to it said, 'No more twist'. The tailor could not understand how the work had been done so he put the waistcoat in his window with a sign 'Come to Prichard where the waistcoats are made at night by the fairies!'.

Beatrix Potter was fascinated by the story for she delighted in fairy-tales. She changed the fairies to mice, the young busy tailor to an old and poor man, and the civic occasion of the Root, Fruit and Grain Society Show to the Mayor's Wedding.

In Gloucester she sat on doorsteps sketching streets and buildings, and the ancient archway of Cathedral Close. She visited homes in Stroud to sketch cottage interiors: a bed with hangings, a dresser filled with crockery and a hob fire grate. At Harescombe Grange she used the coachman's son as a model for her tailor. The Tate Gallery chose her original Tailor of Gloucester pictures for an exhibition, and the story has enthralled millions, of all ages, across the world.

The mystery of the waistcoat was later revealed by the tailor's two assistants who had let themselves into the workshop secretly to do their master's work. The tailor, John Prichard, later became a teacher and lived at Haresfield. He died in 1934 and his tombstone records that he was the tailor of Gloucester.

The House of The Tailor of Gloucester is a tiny shop at 9 College Court, built on to the stone wall of Cathedral Close, the fictional home of the tailor. It is a fascinating centre devoted to the Beatrix Potter range of books and gifts. A working model of the mice, a real old-fashioned hob-grate, dresser and tailor's chair are at the back of the shop in a recreated kitchen, faithful to her illustrations. The Gloucestershire Federation of the Women's Institute embroidered the exquisite waistcoat, modelled on the same waistcoat in the Victoria and Albert Museum which Beatrix Potter had used as her model.

The House of The Tailor of Gloucester is open every weekday 9.30 to 5.30 – admission free.

▼ The House of the Tailor of Gloucester in College Court is a transportation into the tale that has enthralled Potter fans of all generations.

▲ An expansive vale view from Haresfield Beacon.

HARESFIELD BEACON
MAP REF: 78SO8208

About three miles north-west of Stroud, Haresfield Beacon, a promontory at the tip of Ring Hill, is perhaps the most notable of the summits along the Cotswold escarpment. A National Trust car park at the north end of Standish Wood allows easy access to the hill.

Haresfield Hill and Beacon are famous as viewpoints from which the Berkeley Vale can be seen as a pastoral panorama. In the middle distance are the silvery waters of the Severn and the dark expanse of the Forest of Dean, both making an impressive backdrop.

From the Severn the lush green pastures and fruitful fields of the vale are rolled out as a carpet, 700 feet below the beacon.

The geological outliers of Robins Wood Hill and Churchdown Hill can be easily spotted either side of the city of Gloucester. A closer look at the narrowing of the isthmus illustrates how Haresfield too has been detached from the limestone mass to become yet one more of the Cotswolds' outlying hills.

Within the wood-edged bulk of Haresfield Hill Romans made use of an ancient hill-fort and stowed away a hoard of some 3,000 coins.

HIDCOTE
MAP REF: 83SP1742

The twin hamlets of Hidcote Boyce and Bartrim are both pretty and evocative of the heart of England. Hidcote derives from Old English *cote* or *cot* meaning cottages and speaks of its smallness from early times; the hamlets are distinguished by the addition of the names of their respective feudal tenants.

It is to Hidcote Bartrim, 4 miles north-east of Chipping Campden and 1 mile east of the B4632, that visitors are drawn, for, secluded down the leafy country lanes, surrounded by its own farm and thatched cottages is Hidcote Manor and one of Britain's most delightful gardens.

A garden of gardens separated by hedges, Hidcote was created early this century by the great horticulturist, Major Lawrence Johnston, and is now in the care of the National Trust. Its 10 acres are carefully planned winter borders and spring slopes, camellia corners and rock banks, terraces and long walks, circles and dells, avenues of pine, lime, oak and holly, and walks where roses ramble, linking the six major gardens, each on a theme of colour, shape or scent.

A Shakespearean production is staged each summer on the Theatre Lawn, and from the top of the garden there are splendid views over the woods and meadows of the valley westward to Bredon Hill.

Close by to the south-east is the thatched stone cottage village of Ebrington with a church dating back to Norman times. To the north-west lie the thatched timber-framed cottages of Mickleton, the home of the Graves family, the most famous of which was Richard – declared to be one of the best writers of the late 18th century.

KELMSCOT
MAP REF: 79SU2499

'. . . And Thames runs chill
twixt mead and hill
But kind and dear
is the old house here . . .'

The old house for which William Morris wrote this poem is Kelmscott Manor, in his own words a 'many-gabled old house built by the simple countryfolks of the long-past times'.

Kelmscot village is, in part, a memorial to William Morris: a stone-carving on the Memorial Cottages, designed by Philip Webb, showing Morris sitting in the home mead under bird-filled trees is itself a work of art; the Morris Memorial Hall, designed by Ernest Gimson, was opened by George Bernard Shaw.

▼ Hidcote garden is backed by its mellowed 17th-century manor house.

LECHLADE
MAP REF: 95SU2199

*'Clear Coln and Lively Leche go
    down
from Cotteswold's plain,
At Lechlade joining hands, come
    likewise to support
The mother of great Thames.'*

Lechlade takes its name from the Leach and its fame from the Thames. It is the cornerstone of south-east Gloucestershire, meeting the old counties of Wiltshire, Oxfordshire and Berkshire on its boundary bridges.
  St John's Bridge, the oldest, on the A417 Lechlade to Faringdon road, has stood since 1228 close to the confluence of the Leach and the Thames. The Augustinian hospital, founded on the site of what is now the Trout Inn, gave its name to the old bridge, the street

▼ Old Wharf warehouse, Lechlade.

▲ Shell-hood porch, Minchinhampton.

leading to it and St John's Lock, marking the highest navigable reaches of the Thames.
  The view upstream is a glorious juxtaposition of brightly-painted boats bobbing busily through the lock amid the pastoral peace of water-meadows, with the 'dim and distant spire' of St Lawrence's church in the background. Shelley composed his *Summer Evening Meditation* in 1815 in Lechlade churchyard, where Sarah, the first wife of Robert Raikes the founder of the Sunday School movement, is buried.
  A monumental brass to a wool merchant, with his feet on a woolsack, pays tribute to the trade upon which the fine 'wool' church was built. Its re-dedication to a Spanish saint was in deference to Katherine of Aragon, who held the manor in the early 16th century.
  The church makes a striking corner-piece to the triangular market-place, which has the main road running across its base. The Old Vicarage rambles along one side, the library and police station, replacing older houses, on the other, ending with the old, maid-haunted, red-brick New Inn.
  Halfpenny Bridge, arching over the Thames on the A361 Lechlade

to Swindon road, was built in the 18th century and has a tiny square tollhouse on the brow. The old wharf below now teems with pleasure craft. Sleek cruisers set off downstream to Buscot and beyond, while creaking rowing-boats weave their own somnolent course upstream to explore the water-weedlands up to the Round House, where the old canal once brought the Severn to the Thames.

MINCHINHAMPTON
MAP REF: 92SO8700

Minchinhampton, a populous medieval parish which stretched between the valleys of Chalford and Nailsworth, became a busy little market town in the mid-13th century. Its development followed closely that of the Cotswold wool and cloth trades. Sheep were farmed on the high plateau pasture lands and the wool was turned to cloth in the mills of the valley bottoms.
  Its early existence accounts for its traditional building style; all is stone-built and all is in unison. The market square has a fine Market House supported on stone columns, there are many fine houses of considerable age, and, something which few places can boast, a Queen Anne post office.
  On the north side is Minchinhampton Common where a crowd of around 20,000 assembled on foot and horseback to hear George Whitefield preach on a hillock in 1743, despite his having been assaulted in the town.
  High up on the plateau, the Common, the second largest in the Cotswolds, is a spacious stretch of primeval England. Selsey Hill can be seen to the south, Haresfield Beacon to the west, and close-cropped turf for as far as the eye can see. Golfers and riders, picnickers and kite-flyers, loose ponies and cattle all make their own ways across the 580 acres, now in the hands of the National Trust.
  The Tingle Stone, with the big hole in its centre through which rickety children were passed by superstitious mothers, stands close to the entrance to Gatcombe Park, the home of Princess Anne where horse trials are annually staged.

MINSTER LOVELL
MAP REF: 79SP3111

Minster Lovell, an enchanting stone and thatch village on a narrow lane off the Burford to Witney road, is a place to linger.

The old church is set above the river and was built by William Lovell, whose effigy in armour is a fine example of 15th-century work in alabaster; but it is the ruins of the manor house which he built that hold the centre-stage.

Stately in its ruin, Minster Lovell manor house must have been splendid in its prime, as can be seen from plans and old engravings which reconstruct its former magnificence.

Francis, 13th Lord Lovell, sought refuge here after fighting for Lambert Simnel. His whereabouts was known only to a trusted servant who met with an accident, leaving his master to die trapped and starved. Repairs to the house in 1708 revealed the skeletons of a man and a dog in a secret chamber.

Tragedy struck again when a young Lovell bride climbed into an old oak chest in one of the manor's many rooms during a game of hide-and-seek as part of the Christmas wedding festivities. The heavy lid closed on her firm and fast, and the coffer became her coffin. The tragic tale has survived the centuries in the ballad 'The Mistletoe Bough'.

A quite different chapter of social history was written on the south side of the main road. Marked Charterville Allotments on the map, the settlement was one of the five Chartist estates founded by the famous radical, Feargus O'Connor, whose lottery plan for house and land ownership startled the Victorians and excites today's historians.

▲ Minster Lovell Mill, set picturesquely on the banks of the Windrush.

MORETON-IN-MARSH

MAP REF: 84SP2032

Only three counties now meet at the old Four Shire stone near Moreton-in-Marsh, a sizeable grey stone market town on the Foss Way in the north Cotswolds.

Originally part of Blockley parish, Moreton derives from 'farmstead on the moor' and gained its affix in the 13th century as *Henmarsh*. An infuriating erroneous interpretation is 'in-the-Marsh'. The *Marsh* is more properly a corruption of *March*, meaning boundary.

The oldest part of the town is settled round the church, originally a chapel of ease for nearby Bourton-on-the-Hill. There was much rebuilding of both St David's Church, with a fine tower of golden ashlar, and the older buildings in Victorian times.

Transport determined the growth of Moreton-in-Marsh more than any other factor. The improvement of the road system, following the course of the Romans' rigidly direct route, brought the coaching trade through and to the town.

However, it was the age of steam that brought Moreton its greatest

▼ Minster Lovell Hall, a romantic monument to a tragic past.

prosperity. The town increased in size by half as much again when the railway opened up new arteries of trade. One of the few horse railways on the Cotswolds opened in 1826 to run from Moreton 16 miles northward to Stratford on its navigable River Avon. Ten years later a branch line opened to Shipston-on-Stour, and 15,000 tons of coal were hauled along these tracks in each of its boom years. Steam replaced horse power in 1889 and by 1904 the line had fallen out of use. An increase in building continues and the town has expanded this century to the east and south.

The centre of the High Street is the Market Hall, sharing its island with the Mann Institute, inscribed with Ruskin's lovely line, 'Every noble life leaves the fibre of it interwoven for ever in the work of the World'. It is fitting that this should be at Moreton, for here is the great fire-fighting training centre.

A curious coincidence to this most modern and advanced service is that Moreton is one of the few places to boast a curfew tower. It has stood on the corner of Oxford Street for four centuries. Curfew dates back to the Norman Conquest when a bell was rung to warn townsfolk to 'cover-fire' for the night. The curfew bell, dated 1633, was rung at Moreton-in-Marsh until 1860.

About 1½ miles to the north-west, on the A44, is Batsford Arboretum. Within its 50 acres are well over a thousand different species of tree, some hundred or so varieties of magnolia and many hundreds of maples.

▲ The enigmatic Devil's Chimney.

THE DEVIL'S CHIMNEY

The most famous landmark of the Cheltenham area is the pinnacle of rock jutting out of the scarp face of Leckhampton Hill, known locally and recorded officially on OS maps as the Devil's Chimney. It is some two miles south of Cheltenham and can be approached from the B4070. The hill was bought by Cheltenham District Council in 1929 and is now scheduled as a Site of Special Scientific Interest for its natural grasslands which make up the 400-acre common.

Leckhampton hilltop quarries had been worked extensively in the 18th century for the building of Georgian Cheltenham, and it was here on the highest range of the escarpment that the first Cotswold railway was attempted. Initially it was a pulley system to get the stone down to the main road and haul empty trucks up. Quarrying the hill was a thriving industry from Victorian times, first using horse-drawn trams, then engine-drawn rail trucks, until 1925.

The reasons for the quarrymen leaving the strangely-shaped column of stone intact are numerous, but the legend is the only one which has stood the test of two centuries.

The well-known saying 'As sure as God's in Gloucestershire' derived from the extraordinary number of abbeys and churches in the county. This annoyed the old Devil, so he hid on the edge of Leckhampton Hill and pulled out great rocks with his pitchfork to throw down on the monks and pilgrims that passed that way. His evil trick was reversed and the rocks fell on top of him, so he lives deep down in the Cotswold limestone below Dead Man's Quarry, the Chimney marking the spot.

The old GWR carriages and platform posters always used the Devil's Chimney to advertise the Cheltenham area. Scores of cyclists would swarm to the spot to have their photographs taken beside it, and the reckless who risked climbing it always left a coin on the cap as a token to Old Nick. The record was 13 people at any one time standing on the top. Climbing the Chimney is now strictly prohibited.

Erosion of this much-loved landmark put it in grave danger of collapse and created such a passionate stir in the press that the Devil has had his Chimney repaired for some £25,000 – few mere mortals maintain such a costly chimney – but the Cotswolds would never be the same without it.

NAILSWORTH
MAP REF: 92ST8499

W H Davis, the super-tramp poet who made Nailsworth his last home, bade us make 'time to stand and stare' – and if one does, there is much to delight the eye and stir the senses.

Unpretentious and honestly workaday, Nailsworth does not conform to the typical Cotswold wool town picture. In the centre of the industrialised Stroud valley are the gaunt grey mills, their wheels now stilled, but brought back to life by the townsfolk, who have turned the old buildings into new enterprises.

What traditional Cotswold architecture there is stands out: gabled Stokes Croft with an oval window in each gable – a Nailsworth speciality – stands beside Chestnut Hill where formerly pack-horses climbed steeply up to the ancient trading routes. Humble weavers' cottages are still to be found along the roadside, and high above the valley, divorced from the clattering mills which built them, are the grand clothiers' houses.

A clock-tower marks the centre of this town of narrow steep streets, but it is the enormous copper kettle, which reputedly holds 82 gallons, hanging from a building in George Street, that strikes a

more original note for it is one of the earliest forms of advertising.

Nonconformity flourished here in the aftermath of the Industrial Revolution, as evidenced by the meeting houses and chapels, all pre-dating the towerless church built five years after Nailsworth became a parish in 1895.

Artists, craftsmen and writers have always been attracted to this area: the original of John Halifax's mill is said to be Dunkirk Mills, the largest mill building in the district; and devotees of that enigmatic contemporary artist-writer Kit Williams will recognise some of his spectacular scenes in the secret corners of the lovely countryside around.

▲ The Copper Kettle of Nailsworth.

NORTHLEACH
MAP REF: 89SP1114

Northleach was built as a market town in the 13th century, on a commercially strategic point on the Foss Way midway between Cirencester and Stow-on-the-Wold.

It was wool that made Northleach famous and its wealthy merchants built a magnificent church on their profits. The Church of St Peter and St Paul is one of Cotswold's outstanding 'wool' churches, and the likeness of the woolmen can be seen on a unique collection of memorial brasses. Notable among them are William

Midwinter, whose transactions are detailed in the Cely papers; Thomas Busshe, Merchant of the Staple of Calais; John Taylor, with his 15 children, and John Fortey, with his initials in a medallion border.

The market-place stands east of the church and has many 16th- and 17th-century features in the old wool houses and inns lining the High Street.

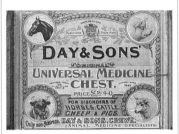

▲ A Northleach Collection exhibit.

At the crossroads on the Foss Way is the Countryside Collection. A museum which has gained several awards since its opening, it makes splendid use of the old 'house of correction'. Built around 1789 by Sir Onesiphorus Paul, the building is a superb illustration of a prison of the period, and the important Lloyd-Baker agricultural collection is one of the best of its kind in the country. Educational facilities bring to life the old courtroom and original cells.

PAINSWICK

MAP REF: 86SO8609

*'Painswick maidens shall be true
Till there grows the hundredth
yew.'*

Legends abound at Painswick, and centred around the impressive colonnades of yew trees in the churchyard of St Mary's is the tradition that only 99 yews will grow at any one time – the Devil always killing off the 100th. So interwoven have they become in 200 years that it is impossible to count the individual trees.

The annual Clipping Ceremony (from the Saxon *ycleping*, meaning embracing) takes place on the Sunday on or following 19th September. The congregation of the open-air service join hands and encircle the church during the singing of the special Clipping Hymn.

The church was damaged by fire and vandalism during the Civil War, and cannon-ball marks are still visible below the clock-face on the tower. Around the church is a collection of Renaissance-style table tombs, designed and carved by a local family of masons, Joseph Bryan and his sons, John and Joseph. John's own tomb is inscribed 'carver'. The lych-gate was built with old belfry timbers and is decorated appropriately with bells and music. At the south-east entrance to the churchyard are the iron 'spectacle' stocks.

Painswick is a fine example of how size has nothing to do with stature, for this old market town is little larger than a village. Its earliest charter was granted in 1253 and New Street was set aside for development as the borough. Parallel to New Street, which was old in 1400, is Friday Street, speaking of an early market and

the delightful Tibbiwell with buildings full of character sloping steeply to the old mill valley.

Bisley Street was the original main street, and the oldest buildings, showing their ancient ties with the wool trade in a name or pack-horse entrance, complete the square as the road divides eastward to Cheltenham, northward to Gloucester.

About a mile to the north is the beauty spot and viewpoint of Painswick Beacon, some 250 acres of common land on the escarpment, crossed with footpaths, a golf course and an Iron Age hill-fort, overlooking the Gloucester and Severn Vale.

PRESTBURY

MAP REF: 87SO9723

The most haunted village of the Cotswolds is one of Prestbury's claims to fame.

It lies under the great bluff of Cleeve Hill: a pretty place so close to Cheltenham as to be counted mistakenly as a suburb, except that there is nothing suburban about Prestbury, for it has an old-world charm and identity of a long-established village in its own right.

Its roots go back beyond Domesday and its name means 'the priests' fortified place'. In 1249 Prestbury was granted a borough charter but did not expand into a

▲ Pearl-grey, stone-built Painswick.
◄ Painswick's legendary yew walk.

prosperous market town owing to its close proximity to Cheltenham.

Cheltenham leased the steeplechase course at Prestbury Park in 1823 and has achieved fame ever since for the races under its own name. The legendary Fred Archer trained here and lived at the King's Arms, a pretty timbered inn. A shoe from one of his horses is preserved in the bar. The first ever Cheltenham Gold Cup was won by Spectre in 1819, earning 100 guineas for its owner. The National Hunt Festival is reckoned to be second only in scale of operation to the British Open Golf Championship, the racegoers consuming some 2,700 gallons of champagne to celebrate their winnings. History has it that the festival evolved indirectly from the long stay in Cheltenham of 'Farmer' George III. Today it is the Queen Mother who sets the royal seal on both the races and the village of Prestbury where she now, traditionally, stops at the thatched bakery to receive a customary box of chocolates and bouquet.

PRINKNASH ABBEY
MAP REF: 86SO8713

'It stands on a glorious but impracticable hill, in the midst of a little forest of beech and commanding Elysium', wrote Horace Walpole of Prinknash in 1774.

Prinknash Abbey, built in 1972 in glowing golden stone quarried at Guiting, stands in starkly simple modern style in the lush countryside beneath the west escarpment. It is in direct architectural contrast to the mellowed manor house on the hill some half-a-mile away, which had served the Benedictine monks for almost half a century.

It was while digging the foundations for the new monastery that the rich beds of clay were discovered which started the famous Prinknash Pottery. From the humble beginnings of making pots in a garden shed to modestly supplement the community's income, the pottery has become the Abbey's major financial support, employing local people and exporting all over the world. Incense and vestments, stained glass and ironwork are also made at Prinknash, and the crypt, consecrated as the Abbey church, is almost entirely furnished by the craft work of the monks.

Magnificent views over the Severn Vale can be seen from the Regency-walled monastery garden, which is open to the public.

RANDWICK
MAP REF: 78SO8206

The hills around are studded with barrows, long and round, and earthworks of the first settlers in this delightful wooded western edge. The valleys are dotted with mills and tiny villages which once eked out a meagre living in the cloth-making industry.

Randwick is just one of the many Stroud valley villages with a tale to tell of just how hard was the hard life: one Randwick son who became Regius Professor of Arabic at Oxford had, as a child, started weaving at 4 a.m. each day and did not finish until 10 p.m.

Poverty-stricken villagers welcomed the zealous arrival of Nonconformist missionaries. George Whitefield attracted over 2,000 to his service at Randwick and wrote that 'by taking down the window behind the pulpit' those in the churchyard could hear.

The old church on the hill attracts a crowd today to celebrate the ancient Randwick Wap. The first ceremony, held on the first Sunday in May, is the cheese-rolling. Three cheeses are carried to the church on flower-decked litters, blessed at a short service,

▲ Making merry, mayor-making at Randwick May-time Wap.

rolled three times anti-clockwise round the church, then cut up and distributed by officers in costume.

The second part of the Wap, held on the second Saturday in May, is the mock mayor-making – a colourful and curious ceremony, which, like the cheese-rolling, dates back to medieval times and enlivens life in a small Cotswold village.

THE RISSINGTONS

MAP REF: 91SP1917 to
91SP1921

Belonging to the north of the central wolds, on the rolling hillside and in the valleys in between, the Rissingtons put down their farming roots and came to terms with their windswept fieldscape 1,000 years ago.

Great Rissington has two village greens: a three-cornered patch to which the main street runs uphill, and a square further to the north-west where the road divides. In the south-west corner is settled the group of church, rectory, manor and farm from which its history emanated.

Little Rissington is a mile away. The house and hangar complex on the high wold road was once famous as the Central Flying School – the Cotswold nest from where the Red Arrows aerobatic team flew. Many of the airmen came back to Little Rissington to be buried in the peaceful spot on the hill where the little Church of St Peter's stands in isolation apart from its village.

Wyck Rissington another mile away lies at the foot of a steeply winding hill. The sweeping Cotswold stone roof of St Laurence is glimpsed from every bend. Full of character, the church can boast having had Gustav Holst as organist. His house faces the horse-grazed village green, which is the central point of this small farming community.

THE ROLLRIGHTS

MAP REF: 85SP2930 to
85SP3231

Legend has locked the Rollright Stones so firmly into the north-east Cotswold landscape that they carry their fabled names on the Ordnance Survey maps, an honour which their more famous Avebury cousins have not achieved.

Rollright, in a corrupt form of Roland the Brave – the legendary champion of Christianity – appears in Domesday, but the hoary old stones on the side of the road between Great and Little Rollright villages assumed their identity in medieval myth.

A king of old, setting out to conquer all England, strode up the hill and was halted by a witch who forecast that after taking seven long strides,

*'If Long Compton thou canst see,
King of England thou shalt be.'*

'Stick, stock, stone,' replied the aggressor, but as he stepped forward to survey his easily won kingdom his view of Long Compton was blocked by a long mound of earth. The witch turned the king and his men into stones and herself into an elder tree. The Whispering Knights, separated from the King's Men because they were whispering together plotting treason, also stand as monolithic reminders of a powerful past.

Long Compton, straggling along the A34 in its hollow below, has a fascinating lych-gate, with a room on top roofed with thatch.

▼ The King's Men, solidified in time and rhyme of the Rollrights.

SEZINCOTE

MAP REF: 84SP1731

Sezincote is an experience, not a village. A victim of the early enclosure system, the village of Sezincote, which had supported a community of 12 plough teams at Domesday, had lost its church benefice to its neighbouring village of Longborough by 1750. Of its parish only a couple of farms remain. It is the house and garden which attract visitors to seek out this quiet place off the A424 Stow-to-Broadway road.

A cultural shock, sited as it is in Cotswold's central wolds, is the Indian-inspired mansion remodelled on an earlier building. Designed by Samuel Pepys Cockerell for his brother, Sir Charles, who made a fortune in the East India Company, Sezincote was visited by the Prince Regent in 1807 and gave him the inspiration for the Indianisation of the Brighton Pavilion.

To heighten the fantasy of the building and authenticate the colour of its material, the native stone was stained to impart a more Indian orange tone. The drive to the house is over an Indian-style bridge by Thomas Daniell, an expert artist in oriental design.

COTSWOLD STONE

The Cotswolds are part of a limestone belt which stretches from Dorset in the south to South Yorkshire in the north-east. In the Bath area the stone is a honey-gold colour. Further north at Painswick the white stone weathers to grey. At Chipping Campden and Broadway a deep golden colour is usual. The variety of colours results from the varying quantities of iron present in the stone. On the high Cotswold hills the topsoil is usually only 6–12 inches deep and small loose limestone rocks are often seen on newly ploughed fields.

A few feet down stone can be quarried for wall building. Cotswold fields were first extensively walled in the 18th and 19th centuries, after the Enclosure Acts were introduced. Many walls are very old, but during a hard winter, frost may break up the stone and the walls will collapse. New stone walls can be seen along boundaries of roads such as the Northleach bypass. The stone is laid in courses and is protected on the top with *combers* (upright stones) which help to keep the wall dry. Years ago small farm cottages were built of this rough stone held together by mortar.

At a lower level in the quarry oolite freestone is found. When first quarried it is soft enough to be sculpted into window surrounds, mouldings and decorative motifs. Many examples of this beautiful work can be seen in the Cotswold wool churches – Fairford, Cirencester and Northleach are among the finest. Smooth-surfaced blocks called ashlar are cut for building. Good examples can be seen at Painswick, Chipping Campden and Minchinhampton.

Cotswold stone roofing slates are made from limestone blocks which split easily along the bedding plane when exposed to frost. Trimmed slates vary from 6–24 inches in depth and are graduated and overlapped from eave to ridge. The slates are held in place on the roof batten by oak pegs through a hole in the top of the slate. The different sizes have delightful names: Short Cock, Muffity, Short Bachelor, Short Wibbuts to mention just a few. Not many quarries are worked today, but all over the Cotswolds abandoned workings can be seen in large fields near villages. The building stone for many Oxford colleges and St Paul's Cathedral in London came from Taynton near Burford.

Today, quarried stone is too expensive for most new houses, and coloured concrete or a mixture of sand and crushed stone is used to make blocks. Roofing slates are now moulded in concrete to look like stone. Most modern houses in the Cotswolds still follow the traditional style of architecture.

▼ The craft of dry-stone walling is to interlock 'one over two'.

▲ Sezincote house, conspicious Indian inspiration in stunning symmetrical architecture.

A temple-pool and shrine are at the head of the little valley, delightfully landscaped with the water-garden by Humphrey Repton, which attracts visitors throughout the year to its trees of unusual size.

THE SHIPTONS

MAP REF: 88SP0318

Often it is only the melancholic bleat of sheep that breaks the silence of the Shiptons in the wilder wold country above the headlands of the Coln valley. The cluster of Shiptons on the high ridge off the A40 Cheltenham-to-Oxford road still accords closely with the sheep farmsteads of Saxon times.

Shipton and its twins, Oliffe and Solers, had a complicated division of lands owned by their respective patrons but were united as one parish in 1776; their former identities were distinguished by locating their churches.

St Oswald belongs to Shipton Oliffe, a small church with a beautiful bell turret made even prettier by tiny pinnacles. Inside are the remains of wall-paintings and early Norman work. The sanctuary is pannelled with oak from old pews discarded by its sister village Solers.

Shipton Solers also has a pretty church. It stands in a garden-like graveyard cleared of gravestones. One of its windows has a curious composition of a Cotswold house, corn sheaves and a ship. It may be that it is symbolic of Christianity sailing forth; if it was meant as a rebus, then the designer failed to understand the local dialect where 'ship' translates as 'sheep'.

There are yet two other Shiptons – Moyne is also in Gloucestershire, but not of Cotswold character; the other is Cotswold, but in Oxfordshire, anciently tied to Wychwood.

▼ Shipton-under-Wychwood's centre-piece is its wide village green.

SHIPTON-UNDER-WYCHWOOD

MAP REF: 91SP2717

Wychwood Forest, one of the five forests recorded in Domesday, gave the poachers on the Oxfordshire edge of the Cotswolds more venison in a week than a London alderman could afford in a year. Mid-Victorian enclosures finally reduced the vast forest to sparsely wooded outcrops, but the name remains.

Shipton – the sheep farmstead – was actually in the forest and a lively place when it was invaded by all and sundry for the great Wychwood Fair.

The focal point is the village green, given to the villagers by a local man, on which a monolithic memorial to those lost in a sea disaster stands. At the far end, sheltered by trees, is the church. The sign of the Shaven Crown, swinging outside the honey-coloured inn on the roadside above the green, catches the eye. Two projecting gabled wings flank a central hall, and lead-paned mullioned windows and a Tudor carriage entrance complete a pleasing picture. Few inns can match its record of serving travellers for six centuries, for it was first licensed in 1384. Its sign showing a monk's tonsure is possibly unique in all England and goes back to its monastic roots when it was a guesthouse for Bruern Abbey. In its long history it has served as medieval hospital, Tudor hunting lodge and a World War II army prison. Elizabeth I presented it to the parish on condition that it continued to be used as an inn.

The village is one of the few remaining to have its own railway station. At the old boundary where Shipton met with Widford and Fulbrook a lone oak tree was where two of the Dunsdon brothers were hanged in chains 200 years ago. Tom, Dick and Harry terrorised the highways with verve and flamboyance far beyond that of the fabled Dick Turpin.

▲ Snowshill, built on a high wolds hill, basks in summer sunshine.

THE SLAUGHTERS

MAP REF: 90SP1523 to
90SP1622

The two small villages of Upper and Lower Slaughter stand on the little Eye stream which meets the Dikler to swell the waters of the Windrush. Slaughter is thought to have been the ancient name for either the stream itself or the slough (mire) caused by it.

Upper Slaughter was the home of a family called Slaughter in the 16th century, but the site has been inhabited since early times. A castle mound is just west of the river but has not been fully excavated. The village is completely unspoilt; an open square is bordered by cottages remodelled in 1906 in keeping with the Cotswold style and using local stone. The practical little bridges over the stream fringed with wild flower-filled grasses and the sounds of the countryside keep this small spot special.

Lower Slaughter downstream is the pretty sister. Here the water is a feature flowing broad and shallow between the neatly-mown grass banks.

There are many good houses with original features but much rebuilding of older cottages. Close regard has been paid to the overall unity because traditional stone has been used. The red brick-built corn mill with its tall chimney and water-wheel makes an attractive corner.

SNOWSHILL

MAP REF: 83SP0933

An isolated little hill village where winter snows lie longest is Snowshill, just east of the north scarpline and three miles south of busy Broadway. An unpretentious place with a history stretching back over 1,000 years, the manor was given by the King of Mercia to the Abbey of Winchcombe and remained in monastic hands until the Dissolution when it was held by the Crown.

Snowshill manor house first attracted attention in 1604. The story of how Ann Parsons was abducted from Elmley Castle to be married secretly at midnight on St Valentine's Eve has been well documented and gives an aura of romance to Ann's Room – an upper part of the great hall.

Now owned by the National Trust, Snowshill Manor is a delightful combination: a traditional Cotswold manor house, built of local stone dating back to around 1500; a terraced garden full of old-fashioned roses, shrubs and ponds; and a collection of which Queen Mary said that the most remarkable part was the collector. Charles Paget Wade amassed all kinds of curios of yesteryear in the manor house, while he lived in a cottage where he refused any modern amenity and slept in a Tudor cupboard-bed.

Beyond the manor house, the village, little more than a closely-knit clutch of old cottages and a tiny rebuilt church, edges the village green and spills down the hill, from which ancient tracks radiate to even smaller Laverton and Buckland in the wooded valley below.

▼ Upper Slaughter Church has a chapel as a memorial to its diarist rector, Francis Witts.

SOUTH CERNEY AND THE COTSWOLD WATER PARK

MAP REF: 94SU0596

It lies south of Cirencester, on the Gloucestershire–Wiltshire border where the gentle hills of Cotswold country meet the water meadows of the Upper Thames valley. Cerney relates to the Churn stream on

▲ Wildfowl are attracted in wide variety to Cotswold Water Park.

which the village stands, but the waters for which South Cerney is known are of its gravel pits.

Gravel has been extracted from the Upper Thames watershed since the 1920s but it was 40 years before plans were made to use the water-filled pits as a recreational resource. The south-eastern dip slope had none of the large open commons of the western scarp lands so the plan to designate a water park centred around South Cerney and reaching in a chain of lakes eastward to Lechlade was welcomed for inland water sports. There are now over 100 lakes and two country parks, nature reserves, picnic areas, holiday lodges and caravan and camping pitches. The two largest areas covering some 24 square miles are fully established south of South Cerney.

The Cotswold Water Park offers water sports, angling and sailing; to the east the Cotswold Leisure Centre at Somerford Keynes extends its facilities to windsurfing and guided tours around the lake reserves in a launch to observe the aquatic wildlife.

Lakeside walks and horse-riding along the disused rail line around South Cerney is in landscape typical of a lowland river valley with wetland flora and fauna – attracting nightingales in the summer, and heron, grebe, lapwing and warbler among the sedge and sallow, rush and willow. Walks along the towpath of the old Thames and Severn Canal radiate from and to Cerney.

The village itself retains its Cotswold heart, despite an expansion of new building.

Unusual in having three manors, South Cerney also delights in unusual names: Bow-Wow is a pleasant walk close to the Old George Inn; Upper Up, now adjoining the village, is a reminder of the days when it was an outlying farming hamlet.

The village is on a long street plan; several houses in Silver Street date back to the 17th century, and Edwards College at the north end, built in Victoria's age as a home for clergy widows, is a fine composition of Tudor-Gothic style. A row of gabled cottages with mullioned windows are in Station Road. The church is large with a Norman tympanum and part of a fine wood crucifix, thought to be the earliest piece of wood-carving in the country.

STANTON

MAP REF: 82SP0634

The perfect Cotswold village – nothing has been allowed to spoil the simple classic lines of Stanton thanks to the foresight of the architect, Sir Philip Stott, who

▼ A vignette of the vernacular Cotswold style at Stanton.

owned the estate from 1906 to 1937.

It lies about 3 miles south-west of Broadway and takes its name from *stan* (stone) farmstead. The long main street is lined with beautiful houses, and nowhere can the local stone and style be seen in such a homogeneous composition.

Tucked behind the village cross on its medieval base is St Michael's Church. It has the feel of age but there is much that is new. Sir Ninian Comper 'signed' his work in one of the windows with a wild strawberry; it was he who reset the ancient glass of the east window, removed from Hailes Abbey and broken by Civil War soldiers who were locked in the church.

The steady tread of centuries has worn down the stone-flagged floor, and under the organ loft, also Comper's work, are medieval pews, their poppy heads gouged deep from the days when shepherds took their dogs to church and fastened them to the pew heads.

The road divides at the northern end, curving round a picturesque spot still known as Sheppey Corner from the age when flocks were shepherded off the hills to the manor's farm for shearing.

STANWAY
MAP REF: 82SP0632

As with Stanton, Stanway takes its name from the local *stan* (stone), but here it is golden and deeply rich like a peach.

The village clusters close to its manor, Stanway House. The gatehouse, breathtakingly beautiful, was long supposed to have been built by Inigo Jones, but is more likely to have been the work of Timothy Strong of Little Barrington. It is an architectural gem: the huge oak doors are carved with birds, and the scallop shell crest of the Tracys surmounts each of the three shaped gables above the roof line.

Stanway owes its precious cohesion of architectural unity and close-knit community living entirely to the manor. It is in the house, an exquisite Jacobean manor with its great hall lit by a window reaching almost to the eaves, its old library, romantic rooms, great passages and little

Picture-book charm at Stanway. ▶

▼ Stunning as a stage set, Stanway House gatehouse was probably the work of a Cotswold mason.

lobbies, that the import of such an ancient lordship is realised. Its distinction lies in its domesticity, for it is, as shown, a typical squire's home furnished and furbished with the stuff of the families who have owned Stanway for centuries. Notable for having changed hands only once, other than by inheritance, in the last 1,260 years (when it was bought at the Dissolution), it is unique in its rent audits at which its tenants appear in person.

Within the grounds and behind the church, is the magnificent tithe barn, built about 1370 in which the great and little tithes were stored for the Abbots of Tewkesbury, in whose charge the manor was at that time. Today it serves as an incredibly beautiful hall in which music and art festivals are held, as well as the local flower show.

A thatched wooden cricket pavilion, set on staddle stones to keep it off the wetland field, was given to the village by Sir James Barrie and marks one end of the village. The war memorial at the other end is a splendid bronze sculpture of St George and the Dragon.

STOW-ON-THE-WOLD
MAP REF: 91SP1925

'Stow-on-the-Wold, where the wind blows cold', runs the age-old jingle. Windswept throughout the centuries, Stow at nearly 800 feet, is the highest town in the Cotswolds.

Henry I granted borough status to Edwardstow. The receiving of the royal charter in 1107 is portrayed on the headstones of the market cross. St Edward is commemorated in the church dedication, an Elizabethan grammar school, an 18th-century house facing the cross and a Victorian hall in the centre of the market square, but has been dropped from the name of the town.

All Cotswold roads lead to Stow, they say; eight intersect here, which must make it one of the easiest places to find. On the path of the ancient ridgeway, the town centre is effectively bypassed by the Roman Foss Way, leaving it free of passing traffic. It is one of the few places without a museum or obvious tourist attraction, but the seeker of the unusual will delight in the Doll's Hospital and private collection of Lillian Middleton, whose beautifully designed and dressed dolls are actually made on the premises. That tourists are attracted to Stow is reflected in the number of inns and tea-shops, pubs and hotels jostling for space around the square and down its narrow alleys, by its old almshouses and behind its ancient stocks.

Stow Fair, where some 20,000 sheep would change hands at a time, is still held twice a year but is now rooted firmly in the Cotswold calendar as Stow Horse Fair. In May and October the long street is filled with horses and ponies, dealers, buyers and country-loving folk.

▲ The old meat market at Stroud has now diversified its trade.

STROUD
MAP REF: 92SO8505

Most guidebooks gloss over Stroud, for it is the five valleys converging upon it and the old mills that punctuate its past and give character to its present that are the more attractive features.

Haphazardly built on steep hills of a spur above the River Frome, Stroud itself scores few marks for architectural merit, but it is a working town rather than a tourist haunt and so is remarkably free of quasi-quaint inns and antique shops. Its past is tucked away in a museum, housed in a Victorian building in Lansdown.

Stroud makes no effort to trade on its heritage as the west of England cloth-making centre. Stroudwater scarlet and Uley blue blazoned its fame abroad as military uniforms, but of the 150 mills which once worked the waters of the Frome and its tributaries only a couple are producing cloth today. Wealthy clothiers chose to build their grand houses on the outskirts of the town, but there is still character to be sought out in its steep and narrow streets.

The Shambles, the old meat market, and the Tudor Town Hall form a charming corner by the parish church. The dignified building, boldly inscribed Stroud Subscription Rooms, accommodates the artistic and social life, while Stratford Park just outside the town offers sports and recreation at its 56-acre leisure centre.

▲ Elegant Georgian terrace leads to Stroud Parish Church.

▼ Stow-on-the-Wold retains its old charm as well as its stocks.

▲ A wide range of activities and arts centre on Sudeley Castle.

SUDELEY CASTLE
MAP REF: 82SP0327

A castle has stood at Sudeley since the time of Ethelred the Unready; the present castle dates back to the mid-15th century when it was rebuilt by Ralph Boteler on the spoils of Henry V's wars.

On approaching the west arch the Portmare Tower on the right is named after the French admiral whom Boteler held prisoner there, using his ransom money to pay for the extensions to the castle.

Queen Katherine Parr, widow of Henry VIII, brought her court to Sudeley on her marriage to Sir Thomas Seymour and is buried in the adjacent St Mary's Chapel. The chapel was desecrated by Cromwell's army, and the castle suffered extensive damage. The ruins of the Elizabethan banqueting hall stand testimony to the violence and scale of the Civil War which had made Sudeley 'the prize of all the buildings in those days'.

A thousand years of history are stored in this castle. Extensive areas of rooms and gardens are open to the public, filled with fascinating reminders of its chequered past. Europe's largest private collection of toys, arms and armour, antiques, fine paintings and an assemblage of Victoriana are the legacy of Emma Dent, a generous benefactor of Winchcombe, to whom the restoration of the castle is due.

Building on the initiative of her predecessor, the current Lady of the Castle has added a further dimension to its attractions by creating a suite of craft workshops within the castle itself. Originally the craftsmen were directly involved with its refurbishment, but now produce high quality items and undertake commissions for the general public, with most subjects reflecting the history of the castle. One is immediately struck by the beautifully written signs and discovers that the calligraphist is also one of the resident craftsmen. Together with textile artists and furniture makers, prestigious exhibitions ensure plenty to see.

TETBURY
MAP REF: 92ST8993

'The design is entirely free from ostentation.' The description applies equally to the market town of Tetbury as it does to Highgrove, one of the most famous addresses in the British Isles.

Highgrove, the home of the Prince of Wales, a substantial country estate, was built in the 18th century for the Pauls, Huguenot immigrants who became prosperous clothiers. They gave to history Sir George Onesiphorus, the famous prison reformer, and Kitcat, the cricketer, who, in 1896, added 193 runs to the 301 of the legendary W G Grace, which is still the Gloucestershire record for the ninth wicket.

Careful park planning by a later owner ensured a clear view across the fields to see the slender spire of Tetbury's Gothic-styled church. St Mary's was rebuilt in 1781, using bits of medieval glass in its incredibly large windows. The town's long history is presented in the heritage centre in the south ambulatory. Housed in the cells of the old court house is the Police Bygones Museum – a fascinating collection of police memorabilia.

The ancient Town Hall, set on its pillars is a notable landmark. Tetbury's market-place adjoining the main thoroughfare was laid out by 1200 and all streets lead to it. At the north end is the Snooty Fox, a Jacobean-style building rebuilt last century to provide a ballroom on the first floor for the Beaufort Hunt. The Chipping, a lesser market, is beyond, with ancient remains of its brief period as a Cistercian priory. Chipping

▼ Despite a bustling town face, Tetbury keeps its country character in quiet steeply-stepped streets, such as the medieval Chipping.

Steps are also of early medieval origin. There are many houses of some architectural merit in the town, but it is Gumstool Hill which is the focus of attention each year for this is where the celebrated Woolsack Races are held on the Monday of Spring Bank Holiday.

The agony of Gumstool Hill, taking its name from the old gumstool – or ducking stool – which once stood at the bottom, is a series of relay races up the one-in-four gradient between the Royal Oak at the bottom of the hill and the Crown at the top, carrying a 48lb sack of wool. Ladies' teams have slightly lighter loads. The modern races, started in 1972, grew out of a tradition of the 17th century when Tetbury was a thriving wool centre and the young drovers performed the feat to impress the young womenfolk of the town. A huge street fair fills the centre of the town, with strolling players and steam organ setting the scene for the only woolsack races in the world.

Just one and a half miles away, Chavenage House – a beautiful Elizabethan mansion – is open to the public.

HISTORIC HOUSES AND GARDENS

The Cotswolds are rich in houses historically interesting for either their architecture, the role they played in some colourful event of the past, or for their inhabitants.

The strongest contender for the title of the oldest inhabited house in England is Horton Court in the south wolds. The Norman hall, now the north wing of the house, was built around 1140 — one of the few known domestic and unfortified houses of that date.

In the north wolds is Buckland Rectory, thought to be England's oldest and most complete medieval parsonage. Stone-built, with a most impressive hall with open timber roof, it dates back to the 15th century.

Chastleton House, near Stow-on-the-Wold, keeps a secret room in its early Jacobean walls, where a fugitive from the Battle of Worcester hid when Cromwell's soldiers stormed the house. Robert Catesby, a conspirator in the Gunpowder Plot, once owned the estate. Chavenage, near Tetbury, a fine Elizabethan house, has two bedrooms in the south-east wing named after Cromwell and Ireton, who slept there during one of the three sieges on nearby Beverstone Castle.

Owlpen Manor, near Dursley, is Tudor and exemplifies the typical Cotswold manorial grouping which is the nucleus of most villages.

Stanway House is an exquisite Jacobean house, a typical

▲ Viols from the music room of Snowshill Manor, part of its eclectic collection of bygones.

squire's residence, while Daneway House at Sapperton, dating back in part to 1250, was used by Gimson and the Barnsleys, who produced beautiful furniture in the Arts and Crafts revival in William Morris tradition.

Cotswold gardens range from the exotic collections of specialists to the cottage plots whose viewing is advertised only on a handwritten notice to raise funds for a village project.

Hidcote Manor garden was the first garden of outstanding merit to be presented to the National Trust, and Kiftsgate Court, its near neighbour, is renowned for its collection of roses and many unusual plants. A small plot in Leysbourne, off the High Street in Chipping Campden, is a newly-formed memorial garden to Ernest Wilson, whose world-wide travels introduced many of the now common species to the English garden.

The central Cotswolds has the knot and herb, and formal-style kitchen gardens within the overall garden of Barnsley House, designed by Rosemary Verey, the well-known writer and lecturer on English gardens.

At Bourton-on-the-Water two local men established world-famous collections in their own gardens: at Chardwar Manor the garden became the original Birdland, and the whole village was rebuilt, to scale, in the garden of the Old New Inn.

The south wolds has the folly garden at Stancombe Park, near Dursley, and the Italian garden of Westonbirt School, which was the 'nursery' for the great arboretum.

◀ Kiftsgate Court garden, renowned for its roses, was developed by generations of its lady owners.

TEWKESBURY
MAP REF: 80SO8932

An ancient and lovely town on the Avon, Tewkesbury belongs properly to the vale, but so dependent were the early fortunes of so many Cotswold manors on the monastic masters of Tewkesbury that they can scarcely be separated.

Tewkesbury Abbey was a powerful land-owner; its manor spread up and over the hills of the Cotswolds as far as Fairford in the south-eastern corner. The enormous tithe barn which can be seen today at Stanway gives some idea of the volume of great and little tithes stowed there for the abbot; and the fact that rustlers stole 1,000 head of the abbey flock from Stanway in 1340 illustrates the scale on which Tewkesbury Abbey farmed its sheep.

many timber-framed houses which are such an attractive feature of this riverside town.

The wide river and low-lying flood meadows restricted a sprawling growth and resulted in back-filling behind older buildings. The resultant narrow entrances have made Tewkesbury a place of secret alley-ways – an early Baptist chapel is tucked away in one, beyond the shadow of the great abbey.

rights were granted by Elizabeth I, and, although its purpose is no longer for the hiring of servants, it is the largest street fair to be held in Gloucestershire.

WESTONBIRT
MAP REF: 78ST8589

As the Cotswold hills flatten on the south-east side edging the Wiltshire plains, modest farmsteads give way to more palatial parkland and fox-hunting fields and coverts.

The village of Westonbirt, on the A433 some 3 miles south-west of Tetbury, was almost wholly rebuilt further west of its 14th-century church by the incredibly rich

◄ Riverside town of Tewkesbury.

▼ Tewkesbury Abbey boasts the highest Norman tower in England.

The town was already a royal borough by Domesday, and although it participated in the wool industry, it did not rise and fall on its fortunes as smaller hill towns did. Sited on the navigable Avon where it joins the Severn, Tewkesbury had the advantage of river transport years before roads were improved. This was the way the stone came for its mighty Norman abbey, brought from Normandy itself by sea and river.

The abbey is the central focus of the town. It was bought by the townsfolk at the Reformation for £453, and its sturdy tower still dominates the roofscape of the

Preservation of its historic past is strong: a unique terrace of houses, built about 1500, adjoins the abbey graveyard; and a delightful timber-framed house has been restored to house the works of John Moore, who captured the town and its characters in his amusing novels. The decisive Battle of Tewkesbury in the Wars of the Roses is re-enacted at festival time. The battlefield still bears the name of Bloody Meadow, and Gupshill Manor, which accommodated the royal party, still offers its services to today's travellers.

One of the oldest Mop Fairs in the country is held in October; the

Victorian, R S Holford, to allow him the luxury of landscaped gardens on a lavish scale. The village, therefore, is interesting as a period-piece but does not follow the concept of traditional Cotswold building.

Westonbirt House was designed by Lewis Vulliamy, who had built Holford's Dorchester House (now the Dorchester Hotel) in Park Lane. Architecturally, Westonbirt – an Elizabethan-style palace – is an important survival. It is now a fashionable girl's school.

Its formal Italian-style garden, terraced with rustic walks and lake and filled with many rare and

▲ Old Corner Cupboard, Winchcombe.

exotic shrubs, is sometimes open to the public in the summer. But the legacy of Holford's passion for gardens by the acre is the arboretum.

Westonbirt Arboretum is the largest in the country. A magnificent landscaped collection of trees and shrubs covering some 600 acres, it has been managed by the Forestry Commission since 1956. Springtime at Westonbirt means rhododendrons and azaleas in glorious profusion and autumn is ablaze with fiery maples.

WINCHCOMBE

MAP REF: 82SP0228

Sheltered under the bluff of the north-west hills, the small town of Winchcombe settled in its winding combe long ago in Saxon times. Capital of what was then a separate shire, Winchcombe was the seat of Mercian royalty. Offa built a nunnery here in 790; Kenulf, his successor, founded an abbey in 811 and Kenulf's son, Kenelm, left it a legacy of legend.

Miracles wrought in the name of the young murdered Kenelm made Winchcombe a place of pilgrimage and its abbey rich and powerful. Of the abbey nothing remains today, but St Peter's Church was built close by as a joint venture between the abbot, who was responsible for the chancel, and Sir Ralph Boteler of Sudeley, who built the nave on behalf of the parish.

After the Dissolution the town looked to the land again and began to grow tobacco. Samuel Pepys wrote of the troops being sent 'to spoil the crop', Parliament being more interested in developing its interests in the newly-established outpost of Virginia than in supporting small local economy.

The past has left to Winchcombe some fine old inns, such as the George, where, carved on the doorway, are the initials of Richard Kidderminster, the 16th-century abbot who raised the status of the abbey to 'equal a little university'.

Tudor buildings survive in Hailes Street leading downhill and northward. On the corner of North Street hefty timber stocks stand outside the Folk Museum, which has a fine collection of international police memorabilia and is the tourist information centre.

Abbey Terrace angles off south-westward, the church with magnificently grotesque gargoyles dominating the junction with Gloucester Street. Vineyard Street, with rustic porched cottages and pollarded trees, slopes steeply off southward to cross the Isbourne in which the town scolds were once ducked. Further on lies Sudeley Castle.

A strenuous climb from here over Humblebee How goes to Belas Knap. Car travellers can get within $\frac{3}{4}$ mile of the ancient long barrow by continuing along Gloucester Street, passing the charming Old Corner Cupboard Inn, to follow the well-signposted route up Corndean Lane.

Belas Knap is the finest example of a false-entrance long barrow on the Cotswolds. Constructed with huge slabs of the oolite limestone to form its burial chambers, it is the revetment walls of the thin ragstone which attract attention. For here high up on the westerly plateau, laid completely without mortar, the drystone walling stands as testimony to the Cotsaller's skill at handling his native stone 4,000 years ago.

▲ An arboreal delight in all seasons, Westonbirt is aglow in autumn with maples and acers.

WITNEY

MAP REF: 79SP3509

Weaving the wool grown on the Cotswolds was not confined to its hill settlements. In the flat plain across the Windrush in Oxfordshire, Witney grew up on the weaving industry. A 'fuller's isle' was recorded at Witney in an Anglo-Saxon charter, and there were two fulling mills by 1223.

Developing from the cloth-making industry, blankets were being made in Witney in the 16th century; plentiful supplies of local wool and the purity of the Windrush waters attracted financial support from a group of wealthy weavers who obtained the Charter for the Company of Blanket Weavers in 1711 and built Blanket Hall in 1721.

Witney blankets achieved early fame – coveted by the American Red Indians 300 years ago, they still find a ready export and home market. Industrial technology has drastically changed the working processes in the factories, and other industries attracted to the town have wrought changes in its street plans and facilities.

The low buildings of the old factories, a wide green and a handful of older houses make a pleasant background to its modern urban face. Even older memories are stirred at the September fair, still known as Witney Feast, and tangible reminders of the past are preserved along the road at Cogges Farm Museum.

Devoted to country life and the preservation of agricultural history, displays are housed in farm buildings and the old manor-house. There is nothing static

▲ Witney, synonymous with blankets, warmly welcomes its visitors.

about Cogges; changing exhibitions, country fairs and demonstrations of the many facets of rural life, from sheep-dog competitions to butter-making, keep alive the skills and crafts of yesteryear.

WOTTON-UNDER-EDGE

MAP REF: 78ST7593

The old town of Wotton suffered total destruction in King John's reign when it was put to the torch by mercenaries taking their revenge on the Berkeley estates. Rebuilt, it regained its borough status in 1253, and its tenured plots, each of one-third of an acre, were let for a shilling a year.

The powerful Berkeley family lived a few miles away from the town, and Thomas Lord Berkeley is buried in Wotton Church. Katherine, Lady Berkeley, built a house in 1384 for a master and two poor boys, on the principles of Winchester, so giving Wotton the distinction of having the first school to be founded by a woman. The present school, far removed from those humble beginnings of 600 years ago, still bears the name of that lady of foresight.

▲ Wotton attracted the celebrated pioneers Jenner, Pitman and Rowland Hill.

The Bluecoat School, founded in 1715, is in Culverhay. Isaac Pitman was the first master of the British School, on the corner of Bear Lane, and perfected his *Stenographic Shorthand* while there, teaching it first as a voluntary subject to the boys.

The High Street continues into Long Street, the Tolsey House on the corner making a prominent feature with its copper dragon weather-vane. Long Street leads to Church Street. The 17th-century almshouses and chapel – a bequest of Hugh Perry, who became Sheriff of London in 1632 – are beautiful gabled buildings and much admired for their architectural planning in a market town which has rebuilt according to its needs.

▼ Time has passed by the shady old Butter Cross at Witney.

COTSWOLD ALE AND GLOUCESTER CHEESE

Brewhouses are still to be spotted at the back of some of the older houses where the ales and wines were made for large households before tea and coffee became popular and more readily available. As hard to find are the old cider presses and cheese rooms, but they do exist, mainly on private farms.

The Cotswolds was once a successful wine-growing area and vineyards were established on the gentler hill slopes around the ancient monasteries. A number of newly planted vineyards are just producing their first wine of modern times in the south-western corner of the region.

Cider was brewed for strictly local consumption, and the farm labourers quaffed millions of gallons in the Cotswold harvest fields. When Gimson and the Barnsley brothers were at Daneway House they made 2,000 gallons in one year from their apple crop for sale to the Sapperton farmers. Pears grew better in the vale, and one tree, known as the Great Westbury Pear, once covered one-and-a-half acres; its branches rooted to form another tree.

The only brewery in the Cotswold hills is set in idyllic scenery at Donnington Mill. A family business, started in 1865 and now run by the third generation, Arkell's public houses were originally only within delivery distance of the brewery's horse-drawn dray, which had to allow for catching and harnessing the horse, loading and returning by nightfall. Fifteen pubs are still served with the famous Donnington ale made by traditional methods, all cask conditioned, with secondary fermentation in the cask. Three types are brewed: the strongest Special Bitter Ale, Best Bitter, and Dark Mild Triple X. The distinctive nutty and malty taste of the traditional ale is strengthened by the pure Cotswold spring water that runs under the bank by the side of the lake. It is with regret that the brewery is unable to accept visitors.

Double Gloucester cheese is the county's speciality. Last century some 1,200 tons of cheese was produced annually, but today there is but one registered farmhouse cheesemaker of the traditional Double and Single Gloucester left – in fact, the only one in the world to be making this cheese in the traditional manner. The decline of the Old Gloucester cattle (distinctively white striped

▲ Traditional casking and spring water produce good Cotswold ale.

down the back of their beautiful mahogany coat with white tail and upward curving horns) reduced the very small-fat globule milk on which the richness of the cheese depends. Only 22 herds remained a decade ago and it is still a rare breed, carefully conserved by those who care about our agricultural heritage.

A revival of interest in ancient farming methods has led to a number of small enterprises developing cheesemaking and yoghurt production from ewe's milk. Several milking flocks have now appeared in the Cotswolds – and their cheese can be found in selected local shops.

▼ Donnington hamlet has a picturesque mill powering a private brewery.

FACT FILE

CONTENTS

Places to Visit
Stately homes, castles, gardens, museums, art galleries and other attractions

Sports and Activities
Angling, cycling, golf, riding, walking, watersports

Craft Shops
A selection of workshops producing original items

Useful Information
Addresses, information centres, market days, theatres and cinemas

Customs and Events
A calendar of festivals

▲ The River Windrush flows idly through Bourton-on-the-Water.

PLACES TO VISIT

This is a selection of places to visit in the Cotswolds. Places are listed here under their nearest town or village, and as a rule correspond to the entries in the gazetteer, where, in many cases, there are fuller descriptions.

The opening times given are intended to provide a rough guide only. Very often a place may just open for part of the day or close for lunch. Also, although stated as open all year, many places are closed over Christmas and New Year.

Full information should be obtained in advance of a visit, from the nearest local tourist information centre (see page 74).

Some places are owned either by the National Trust or are in the care of English Heritage, and if this is the case they are accompanied by the abbreviation NT or EH.

BH = bank holiday
Etr = Easter

ASHLEWORTH

Tithe Barn. *Fine 15th-century example.* Open all year, daily.

BIBURY

Arlington Mill. *Folk museum, working mill, rare breeds.* Open Mar to Oct, daily; Nov to Feb, weekends only.

Bibury Trout Farm. *Working farm, shop, gifts.* Open all year, daily.

BOURTON-ON-THE-WATER

Birdland, Rissington Rd. *Penguins, tropical house, free-flying birds.* Open all year, daily.

Cotswolds Motor Museum. *Vintage cars and automobilia housed in water-mill.* Open Feb to Nov, daily.

Folly Farm Waterfowl, 2m from village off A436. *Conservation centre.* Open all year, daily.

Model Railway Exhibition, High St. *Continental and British models.* Open Feb to Nov, daily.

Model Village, Old New Inn. *Replica of Bourton in Cotswold stone.* Open all year, daily.

Village Life Exhibition, The Old Mill. *Edwardian village shop, with forge.* Open Feb to Nov, daily.

BROADWAY

Barnfield Cider and Wine Mill, Broadway Rd. *Cider press, tastings.* Open all year, daily.

BURFORD

Cotswold Wildlife Park, 2m S of Burford. *White rhino, monkeys, butterfly house, reptile house, adventure playground.* Open all year, daily.

BUSCOT

Buscot House and Park (NT). *Fine water-garden and collection of paintings in house.* Open Apr to Sep, Wed to Fri and alternate weekends. Closed BH Mon.

CHEDWORTH

Chedworth Roman Villa (NT). *Fine site, with museum.* Open Mar to Oct, Tue to Sun and BH Mon; Nov to early Dec, Wed to Sun.

CHELTENHAM

Art Gallery and Museum, Clarence St. Open all year, Mon to Sat; May to Sep, daily. Closed BHs.

Gustav Holst Birthplace Museum, Clarence Rd. *Composer's Regency home.* Open all year, Tue to Sat. Closed BHs.

Pittville Pump Room, Museum and Gallery of Fashion, Pittville Park. Open Nov to Mar, Tue to Sat; Apr to Oct, Tue to Sun. Open some BHs.

CHIPPING CAMPDEN

Woolstaplers Hall Museum, High St. *One of the town's oldest buildings housing bygones.* Open Apr to Oct, daily.

CIRENCESTER

Cirencester Park. *Home of the Earl Bathurst.* Open all year, daily.

Corinium Museum, Park St. *Impressive displays of mosaic floors.* Open Apr to Oct, daily; Nov to Mar, Tue to Sun.

FILKINS

Swinford Museum. *Domestic and agricultural bygones.* Open May to Sep, first Sun in month. Other times by appointment.

GUITING POWER

Cotswold Farm Park. *Rare breeds in Cotswold farm setting.* Open Etr to Sep, daily.

HAILES

Hailes Abbey (EH and NT). *Beautiful Cistercian ruin.* Open Apr to Sep, daily; Oct to Etr, Tue to Sun.

HIDCOTE

see Mickleton

MICKLETON

Hidcote Manor Garden (NT). *A series of small gardens famous for rare trees, shrubs and old roses.* Open Etr to Oct daily, except Tue and Fri.

▼ Cotswold Farm Park, Guiting Power.

Kiftsgate Court Gardens. *Superb views and unusual species.* Open Apr to Sep, Wed, Thu, Sun and BHs.

MORETON-IN-MARSH

Batsford Arboretum. *Over 50 acres of rare trees and bronze statues.* Open end March to Oct, daily.

Chastleton House, SE of Moreton off A44. *Jacobean manor with famous long gallery and topiary garden.* Open Etr to Sep, Fri to Sun and BH Mon.

Cotswold Falconry Centre, Batsford Park. *Daily demonstrations.* Open Mar to Nov, daily.

Sezincote, off A4. *Indian-style house with water-garden.* House open May to Jul and Sep, Thu and Fri. Garden open all year, except Dec, Thu, Fri and BH Mon. ▼

NORTHLEACH

Cotswold Countryside Collection, Fosse Way. *Agricultural history housed in former House of Correction – one of the county's 'country prisons'.* Open Apr to Oct, daily.

Keith Harding's World of Mechanical Music, High St. *Collection of music boxes, automata and mechanical musical instruments. Regular demonstrations and tours.* Open all year, daily.

PAINSWICK

Prinknash Abbey Pottery, 2m N of Painswick. *Abbey with pottery worked by local craftsmen.* Open all year, daily.

Prinknash Bird Park, Prinknash Abbey. *Deer park with peacocks, waterfowl, pheasants.* Open Etr to Oct, daily.

Rococo Garden, Painswick House. *Six-acre garden with garden buildings, vistas and woodland paths.* Open Feb to mid-Dec, Wed to Sun and BHs.

SLIMBRIDGE

Wildfowl and Wetlands Trust. *Swans, geese, ducks and flamingoes in 800 acres.* Open all year, daily.

SNOWSHILL

Snowshill Manor (NT). *Manor house with collections of clocks, toys, bicycles, Japanese armour and more.* Open Apr and Oct, Sat and Sun; May to Sep, Wed to Sun and BH Mon.

STANWAY

Stanway House. *Jacobean manor house with unusual furniture.* Open Jun to Aug, Tue and Thu.

STROUD

District Museum, Lansdown. *Local archaeology, folk material, textile history.* Open all year, Mon to Sat. Closed BHs.

SUDELEY CASTLE

See Winchcombe

TETBURY

Chavenage, 2m NW of Tetbury. *Elizabethan house with Cromwellian relics.* Open May to Sep, Thu, Sun and BHs.

Police Bygones Museum, Long St. *Housed in three police cells.* Open Apr to Oct, Mon to Sat.

TEWKESBURY

Tewkesbury Museum, Barton St. *History of the town, model of Battle of Tewkesbury, and Walker Collection of model fairground.* Open Etr to Oct, daily.

The John Moore Countryside Museum, Church St. *Natural history with emphasis on conservation.* Open Etr to Oct, Tue to Sat and BHs.

The Little Museum, Church St. *Cottage built in 1450.* Open Etr to Oct, Tue to Sat and BHs.

WESTONBIRT

Westonbirt Arboretum. *Over 600 acres with fine collection of temperate trees and shrubs.* Open all year, daily.

WINCHCOMBE

Folk Museum, Town Hall. *Includes police uniforms from around the world.* Open Apr to Oct, Mon to Sat.

Railway Museum, Gloucester St. *A hands-on museum of railway relics.* Open all year; daily in summer, weekends only in winter.

▲ Sudeley Castle and Gardens, off A46/B4632. *Fine house with many treasures and extensive gardens.* Open Apr to Oct, daily.

WITCOMBE

Witcombe Roman Villa (EH). *Remains of a large villa, with mosaic pavements.* Open any reasonable time.

WITNEY

Cogges Farm Museum, Cogges. *Edwardian farm with livestock demonstrations, nature and history trails.* Seasonal opening times, closed Mon.

WOTTON-UNDER-EDGE

Newark Park, 1½m E of Wotton. *Elizabethan hunting lodge.* Open Apr, May, Aug and Sep, Wed and Thu.

SPORTS AND ACTIVITIES

The following information is by no means comprehensive and further details can be obtained from the authorities and contacts given.

Addresses are listed under Useful Information on page 73.

ANGLING

Day tickets may be purchased for coarse and game fishing at a number of Cotswold locations. Rod licences are available from the Thames Water Authority.

There are day fishing facilities at Aston Magna Pool, which is part of the Batsford Estate, Moreton-in-Marsh, during the coarse fishing season. Permits are obtainable from the estate office, the fishing tackle shop in Boat Lane, Evesham, or Manders in Shipston-on-Stour.

Fly fishing is available at Donnington Fish Farm, Condicote Lane, near Upper Swell.

See also **Watersports**

CYCLING

Bicycles can be hired at the following establishments in the Cotswolds.

Broadway, *Leedons Park,* Childswickham (0386 852 423).

Moreton-in-Marsh, *Jeffrey Toyshop,* High Street (0608 50756).

Tetbury, *Thames and Cotswold,* 21 Church Street (0666 53490).

Winchcombe, *Anchor Cycles* (0242 602550).

GOLF

Visitors are welcome at the following clubs and courses.

Broadway, *Broadway,* Willersey Hill (0386 853683).

Burford, *Burford,* Swindon Road, ½m S of Burford (099382 2583).

Cheltenham, *Cotswold Hills,* Ullenwood, 3m S of Cheltenham (0242 515264).
Lilley Brook, Cirencester Road 3m SE of Cheltenham (0242 526785).

Chipping Norton, *Chipping Norton,* Southcombe, 1½m E of Chipping Norton (0608 2383).

Cirencester, *Cirencester,* Bagendon, 1½m N of Cirencester (0285 652465).

Cleeve Hill, *Cleeve Hill,* nr Prestbury (024267 2592).

Dursley, *Stinchcombe Hill,* Stinchcombe Hill, 1m W of Dursley (0453 2015).

Gloucester, *Gloucester Hotel and Country Club,* Matson Lane, Robinswood Hill, 2m SW of Gloucester (0452 25653).

Painswick, *Painswick,* 1m N of Painswick (0452 812180).

Tewkesbury, *Tewkesbury Park Hotel Golf and Country Club,* Lincoln Green Lane, 1m SW of Tewkesbury (0684 295405).

RIDING AND TREKKING

Bourton-on-the-Water, *Long Distance Riding Centre,* Mead House, Rissington Road (0451 21101).

Cheltenham, *Southam Riding School,* Southam de la Bere, Prestbury Nr Cheltenham (0242 42194).

Cirencester, *South Cerney Riding School,* Cerney Wick Farm, Cerney Wick (0793 75015).
Talland School of Equitation,

Church Farm, Siddington (0285 2318/2437).

Stroud, *Camp Riding Centre,* Camp (028582 219).

SKI CENTRE

Two main ski slopes through woodland and a nursery slope for beginners are open all year at Gloucester Ski Centre, Robinswood Hill (0452 414300).

WALKING

The **Cotswold Way** between Chipping Campden and Bath and the **Oxfordshire Way** between Bourton-on-the-Water and the Chilterns are long-distance footpaths which can be found in the area. They are well signposted.

There are also several country parks in the area, many of which have nature trails, and a number are described in the gazetteer section of the book.

For information about woodland walking, write to the Forestry Commission.

Details of guided walks in the Cotswolds can be obtained from the Gloucestershire County Council Planning Department. Please enclose a SAE.

WATERSPORTS

Facilities for angling, birdwatching, windsurfing, sailing and other watersports are available at:

Cirencester, *The Cotswold Water Park,* 5m S of Cirencester (0285 861459).
Keynes Park Lakes, Somerford Keynes (0285 861202).

Tewkesbury, *Croft Farm Leisure and Water Park,* Bredons Hardwick (0684 72321).

CRAFT SHOPS

BOURTON-ON-THE-WATER

The Cotswold Perfumery, Victoria St. *Perfumes manufactured on the premises, plus jewellery.*

CIRENCESTER

The Cirencester Workshops, Brewery Court. *Old brewery housing*

independent craft businesses. Open all year, Mon to Sat.

FILKINS

Cotswold Woollen Weavers, between Burford and Lechlade. *Traditional machinery and exhibition. Clothes, furnishings, fabrics for sale.* Open all year, daily.
Cross Tree Gallery, near Lechlade. *Work of contemporary Cotswold artists and craftsmen.* Open all year, Tue to Sat.

MORETON-IN-MARSH

Wellington Aviation Art Gallery, Bourton/Broadway road. *Paintings and prints of aircraft, sculptures, books etc.* Open all year, Tue to Sun.

STOW-ON-THE-WOLD

Henry-Brett Galleries, Park St. *Twentieth-century paintings and sculpture; many mediums.* Open all year, Mon to Sat.

STROUD

Rooksmoor Mills, Bath Rd. *Crafts and gifts from a 19th-century woollen mill.* Open all year, daily.
Selsley Herb and Goat Farm, Water Ln, Stroud/Dursley road. *Herbs, herbal products, pot-pourri etc.* Open Apr to Sep, daily.

TEWKESBURY

Conderton Pottery, The Old Forge, Conderton, 5m NE of Tewkesbury. *Handmade stoneware.* Open all year, Mon to Sat.
Cotswold Collections, Darkes House, Conderton. *Classic ladies clothing in silk, cotton and wool, plus furnishings.* Open all year, Tue to Sat.

WINCHCOMBE

Winchcombe Pottery, N of Winchcombe, off B4632. *Domestic pottery made and sold, plus other craftsmen on site.* Open in summer daily; winter, Mon to Sat.

USEFUL INFORMATION

ADDRESSES

English Heritage (EH) Bridge House, Clifton, Bristol BS8 4XA (0272 734472).

Forestry Commission 231 Corstorphine Road, Edinburgh EH12 7AT.

Gloucestershire County Council Shire Hall, Gloucester GL1 2TN (0452 425674).

Heart of England Tourist Board 2/4 Trinity Street, Worcester WR1 2PW (0905 613132).

The National Trust (NT)
Severn Regional Office, Mythe End House, Tewkesbury GL20 6EB (0684 850051).

Thames Water Authority
Witney STW, Ducklington Lane, Witney OX8 7JH (0993 771171).

TOURIST INFORMATION CENTRES

Those marked with an asterisk are not open during the winter.

Bath, Abbey Church Yard (0225 462831).

Cheltenham, Municipal Offices, Promenade (0242 522878/521333).

Chipping Campden,* Woolstaplers Hall Museum, High Street (0386 840289).

Cirencester, Corn Hall, Market Place (0285 654180).

Gloucester, St Michael's Tower, The Cross (0452 421188).

Northleach,* Cotswold Countryside Collection (0451 60715).

Painswick, The Library, Stroud Road (0452 813552).

Stow-on-the-Wold, Hollis House, The Square (0451 31082).

Stroud, Subscription Rooms, George Street (0453 765768).

Tetbury,* The Old Court House, 63 Long Street (0666 53552).

Tewkesbury, The Museum, 64 Barton Street (0684 295027).

Winchcombe,* Town Hall, High Street (0905 723471, ext 201/2/4).

MARKET DAYS

Markets are a traditional feature of many Cotswold towns, and some of them date back hundreds of years.

Cheltenham (Market Street and Winchcombe Street) Thursday and Saturday

Chipping Norton, Wednesday

Cirencester, Monday and Friday

Gloucester, Saturday

Moreton-in-Marsh, Tuesday

Stroud, Saturday

THEATRES AND CINEMAS

There are theatres at Bath, Cheltenham, Dursley, Gloucester and Tewkesbury, and cinemas at Bath, Cheltenham, Cirencester and Gloucester.

CUSTOMS AND EVENTS

Although the events shown in this section usually take place in the months under which they appear, the actual dates may vary from year to year.

Numerous other events, such as fetes, county shows, flower festivals and horse shows, also crop up regularly.

Full details of exactly what is happening where can be obtained from tourist information centres (see page 74) or local newspapers.

APRIL

St George's Day Mummers and Morris Dancing
Gloucester (23rd)
Celebrations in city centre

MAY

Cheese Rolling Ceremony
Cooper's Hill (Spring BH Monday)
Cheese chased down the hill by local people, for prizes

Randwick Cheese Rolling
Randwick (first Sunday)
Three cheeses rolled round church. Two kept to open the Randwick Wap (below)

Randwick Wap
Randwick (second Saturday)
Procession, fair, dancing

Woolsack Day
Tetbury (last Monday)
Traditional races, plus medieval market and street entertainers

JUNE

Robert Dover's Games
Dover's Hill, Chipping Campden (first Friday after Spring BH)
Tug of war, greasy pole, dancing, fireworks, sideshows

Scuttlebrook Wake
Chipping Campden (first Saturday after Spring BH)
Queen crowned, fancy dress parade, floats, races, morris dancing

JULY

Festival of Music
Cheltenham
Concerts, readings, recitals

AUGUST

Cranham Feast
Overton Farm, Cranham (first Monday after 4th August)
Feast by invitation, with funfair, dancing, sporting events

SEPTEMBER

Clipping Ceremony
St Mary's Church, Painswick (Sunday nearest 19th)
Outdoor service, children wearing garlands join hands round church

OCTOBER

Mop Fair
Cirencester (Monday before and after 11th October)
Funfair

Stow Horse Fair
Stow-on-the-Wold
Traditional fair

Festival of Literature
Cheltenham
Literary events in the town

▼ A highlight of the Runnick Wap at Randwick is the centuries old mock Mayor-making ceremony.

Atlas

▲ Haresford Beacon

The following pages contain a legend, key map and atlas of the Cotswolds, three circular motor tours and sixteen planned walks in the Cotswolds countryside.

MAP SYMBOLS

THE GRID SYSTEM

The map references used in this book are based on the Ordnance Survey National Grid, correct to within 1000 metres. They comprise two letters and four figures, and are preceded by the atlas page number.

Thus the reference for Cirencester appears 93 SP 0201

93 is the atlas page number

SP identifies the major (100km) grid square concerned (see diag)

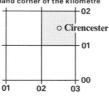

80/81	82/83	84/85
86/87	88/89	90/91
92/93	94/95	

SO SP
ST SU

0201 locates the lower left-hand corner of the kilometre grid square in which Cirencester appears

02 can be found along the bottom edge of the page, reading W to E

01 can be found along the right hand side of the page, reading S to N

o Cirencester

02
01
00
01   02   03

ATLAS 1:63,360 – 1" TO 1 MILE ROADS, RAILWAYS AND PATHS

M 5	Motorway
	Motorway Main road under construction
A 40(T)	Trunk Road
A 429	Main Road ⎫ Single & Dual
B 4019	Secondary Road ⎭ Carriageway
	Narrow Road with passing places
	Road generally over 4m wide
	Road generally under 4m wide
	Minor Road, Drive or Track
- - - - - - -	Path
≫—→	Gradients: 20% (1 in 5) and steeper 14% (1 in 7) to 20% (1 in 5)
	Multiple or Single Track
	Narrow Gauge Track
	Bridges. Footbridge
	Tunnel Cutting
	Freight Line, Siding or Tramway
a b	Station (a) principal (b) closed to passengers
LC	Level crossing
	Viaduct Embankment

PUBLIC RIGHTS OF WAY

-·-·-·-·-·-	Road used as a Public Path
-+-+-+-+-+-	By-way open to all traffic
················	Footpath
- - - - - - -	Bridleway

Public rights of way indicated by these symbols have been derived from Difinitive Maps as amended by later enactments or instruments held by Ordnance Survey on 1st October 1990 and are shown subject to the limitations imposed by the scale of mapping.

Later information may be obtained from the appropriate County Council. The representation in this atlas of any other road track or path is no evidence of the existence of a right of way.

Danger Area   MOD Ranges in the area. Danger! Observe warning notices

BOUNDARIES

Symbol	Description	Symbol	Description
+—·—+—	National	—·—·—·—	County
	National Park	+ + + +	District
NT	National Trust	NT	always open
		NT	opening restricted
FC	Forestry Commission		Pedestrians only – observe local signs

GENERAL FEATURES

Symbol	Description	Symbol	Description
⊥	Radio or TV mast	P	Post Office
		PH	Public House
⌖	Church ⎫ with tower	MP	Mile Post
⌖	or ⎬ with spire	MS	Mile Stone
+	Chapel ⎭ without tower or spire	LDP	Long Distance Path
∘	Chimney or Tower	CH	Club House
⊘	Glasshouse	TH	Town Hall, Guildhall or equivalent
	Bus or Coach Station	PC	Public Convenience (in rural areas)
△	Triangulation Pillar	VILLA	Roman *Castle* Non-Roman
⚡	Windmill	✕	Battlefield (with date)
		☆	Tumulus
⊥	Windpump	+	Site of Antiquity

Symbol	Description	Symbol	Description
	Electricity Transmission Line		
>— —>— —>	Pipe Line		Woods
	Quarry		Orchard
	Spoil Heap or Refuse Tip		Park or Ornamental Grounds

WATER FEATURES

Marsh or salting
Towpath Lock
Aqueduct   Canal   Ford
Normal tidal limit
Lake Weir Bridge
Footbridge
Canal (dry)

HEIGHTS AND ROCK FEATURES

outcrop   cliff   650
600   scree

Contours are at 10 metres vertical interval

·144 Heights are to the nearest metre above mean sea level

Heights shown close to a triangulation pillar refer to the station height at ground level and not necessarily to the summit.

TOURS

2 🚗	Start point of tour		Featured tour
→	Direction of tour	⑥	Point of Interest

TOURIST INFORMATION

Symbol	Description	Symbol	Description
Ⓐ Ⓐ	Camp Site		Nature reserve
	Caravan Site	☆	Other tourist feature
ℹ ℹ	Information Centre		Preserved railway
P P	Parking Facilities		Racecourse
	Viewpoint		Wildlife park
✕ ✕	Picnic site		Museum
	Golf course or links		Nature or forest trail
	Castle	m	Ancient monument
	Cave		Places of interest
	Country park	ℭ	Telephones : public or motoring organisations
	Garden		Public Convenience
	Historic house	▲	Youth Hostel

◆ ◆ Waymarked Path / Long Distance Path

TOURS 1:250,000 – ¼" TO 1 MILE ROADS AND RAILWAYS

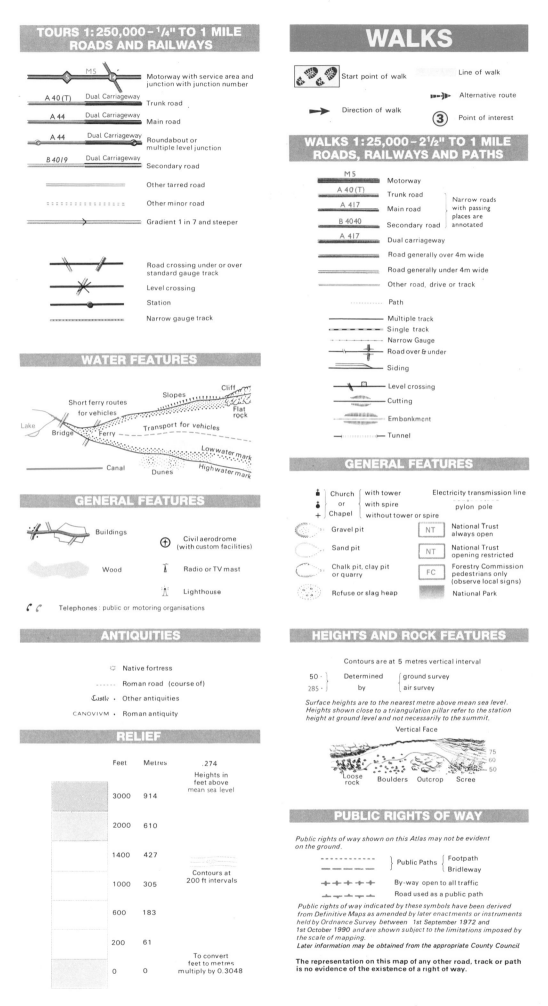

Motorway with service area and junction with junction number

A 40 (T) Dual Carriageway Trunk road

A 44 Dual Carriageway Main road

A 44 Dual Carriageway Roundabout or multiple level junction

B 4019 Dual Carriageway Secondary road

Other tarred road

Other minor road

Gradient 1 in 7 and steeper

Road crossing under or over standard gauge track

Level crossing

Station

Narrow gauge track

WATER FEATURES

Cliff
Slopes
Short ferry routes for vehicles
Flat rock
Lake
Transport for vehicles
Bridge Ferry
Low water mark
Canal Dunes High water mark

GENERAL FEATURES

Buildings

Civil aerodrome (with custom facilities)

Wood

Radio or TV mast

Lighthouse

Telephones : public or motoring organisations

ANTIQUITIES

Native fortress

Roman road (course of)

Castle · Other antiquities

CANOVIVM · Roman antiquity

RELIEF

Feet	Metres
		.274

Heights in feet above mean sea level

3000	914
2000	610
1400	427

Contours at 200 ft intervals

1000	305
600	183
200	61

To convert feet to metres multiply by 0.3048

| 0 | 0 |

WALKS

Start point of walk

Line of walk

Alternative route

Direction of walk

③ Point of interest

WALKS 1:25,000 – 2½" TO 1 MILE ROADS, RAILWAYS AND PATHS

M 5 Motorway

A 40 (T) Trunk road

A 417 Main road } Narrow roads with passing places are annotated

B 4040 Secondary road

A 417 Dual carriageway

Road generally over 4m wide

Road generally under 4m wide

Other road, drive or track

Path

Multiple track

Single track

Narrow Gauge

Road over & under

Siding

Level crossing

Cutting

Embankment

Tunnel

GENERAL FEATURES

Church or Chapel { with tower / with spire / without tower or spire

Gravel pit

Sand pit

Chalk pit, clay pit or quarry

Refuse or slag heap

Electricity transmission line
pylon pole

NT National Trust always open

NT National Trust opening restricted

FC Forestry Commission pedestrians only (observe local signs)

National Park

HEIGHTS AND ROCK FEATURES

Contours are at 5 metres vertical interval

50 · Determined { ground survey
285 · by { air survey

Surface heights are to the nearest metre above mean sea level. Heights shown close to a triangulation pillar refer to the station height at ground level and not necessarily to the summit.

Vertical Face

75
60
50

Loose rock Boulders Outcrop Scree

PUBLIC RIGHTS OF WAY

Public rights of way shown on this Atlas may not be evident on the ground.

} Public Paths { Footpath / Bridleway

+ + + + + By-way open to all traffic

Road used as a public path

Public rights of way indicated by these symbols have been derived from Definitive Maps as amended by later enactments or instruments held by Ordnance Survey between 1st September 1972 and 1st October 1990 and are shown subject to the limitations imposed by the scale of mapping.
Later information may be obtained from the appropriate County Council

The representation on this map of any other road, track or path is no evidence of the existence of a right of way.

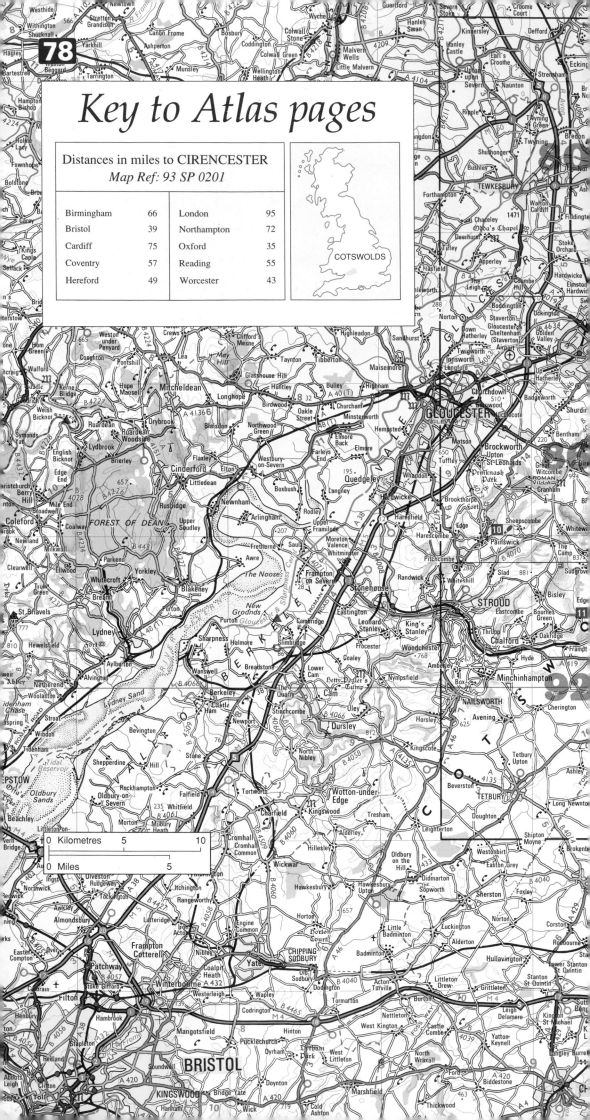

Key to Atlas pages

Distances in miles to CIRENCESTER
Map Ref: 93 SP 0201

Birmingham	66	London	95
Bristol	39	Northampton	72
Cardiff	75	Oxford	35
Coventry	57	Reading	55
Hereford	49	Worcester	43

COTSWOLDS

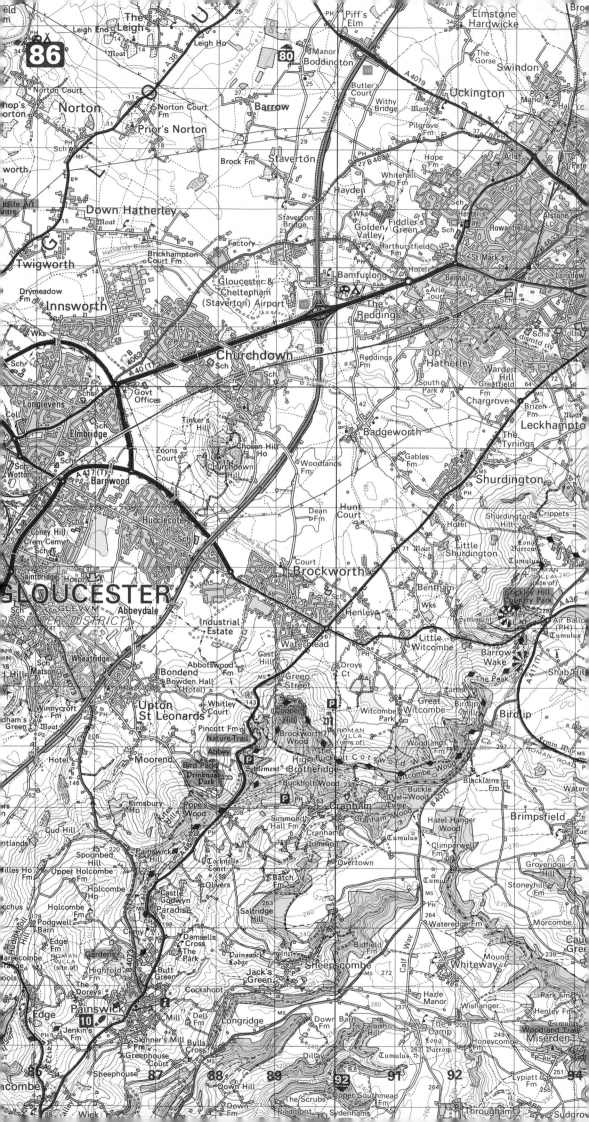

TOUR 1
THE VALE OF EVESHAM

The steep escarpment of the Cotswolds contrasts with the timber and thatch of the Vale of Evesham on this tour. The route veers north for a taste of Shakespeare country and returns via Chipping Campden.

ROUTE DIRECTIONS

The drive starts from Moreton-in-Marsh①. 65 miles.

Follow the Oxford road, A44, for 1¾ miles. Here the road passes the Four Shires Stone where the counties of Gloucestershire, Oxfordshire and Warwickshire (and, before 1931, Worcestershire) meet. After ¾ mile turn right, unclassified road for Chastleton②.

Half a mile on turn left and cross a cattle grid, then at the end turn right, A44. Beyond the Cross Hands public house turn left, unclassified road, signed Rollright. After 2 miles, on the right, lie the Rollright Stones③.

In ¾ mile turn left, A34, signed Stratford, and descend to Long Compton, then continue to Shipston-on-Stour. Turn left, B4035, and after 1¾ miles cross the main road. In 1½ miles keep forward on the unclassified road to Charingworth and Ebrington. At the end of the main street bear right and then right again, signed The Hidcotes. After 2 miles a detour can be made by following signs to Hidcote Manor Gardens④.

Opposite Hidcote, on the unclassified road, is Kiftsgate Court garden⑤.

The main tour turns left, signed Mickleton. In 1 mile turn right and immediately right again, B4632 (formerly A46), signed Stratford, to enter Mickleton. At the end of the village bear left, then in ½ mile go forward, unclassified road, signed Long Marston. Continue through Long Marston to Welford-on-Avon. After crossing the river, turn left, A439, to reach the edge of Bidford-on-Avon.

At the roundabout take the first exit, B4085, signed Broadway, and cross the

15th-century bridge. After ½ mile turn right for Cleeve Prior and South Littleton. One mile beyond South Littleton go over a level crossing, then take the first turning left, unclassified road, to reach Bretforton, where the B4035 is joined, and continue to Weston Subedge.

At the Seagrave Arms turn right, B4632 (formerly A46), signed Cheltenham, pass through Willersley, and in 1¾ miles, at the T-junction, turn right, A44 into Broadway⑥.

By the Swan Hotel turn left, unclassified road, signed Snowshill. Ascend and later bear right into the village of Snowshill⑦.

Turn left at the church, then at the top go forward over the crossroads, signed Chipping Campden and Broadway Tower (care required). After 1¼ miles turn left, signposted Broadway, to Broadway Tower⑧.

In ½ mile cross the main road, signed Saintbury, and pass the Fish Hill Picnic Area. After another ¾ mile turn right, signed Chipping Campden. Continue for 1½ miles and at the crossroads turn right for Chipping Campden⑨.

Leave the town by Sheep Street, B4081, signed Broad Campden, and after ¼ mile turn left, unclassified road, for Broad Campden. In the village turn right then shortly right again and climb to Blockley⑩.

Turn left then shortly right, B4479, signed Moreton-in-Marsh. After 1½ miles, at the T-junction, turn left, A44 to pass through Bourton-on-the-Hill⑪.

Continue on the A44 to return to Moreton-in-Marsh.

POINTS OF INTEREST

① A small, busy town of the northern Cotswolds, Moreton-in-Marsh is on the route of the Roman Foss Way, which forms its wide main street.

② The scenic village of Chastleton contains Chastleton House, a notable Cotswold-stone building dating from 1603.

③ The Rollright Stones are two curious Bronze Age clusters of stones, on the sides of the road between Great and Little Rollright villages, that assumed their identity in medieval myth.

④ Cultivated by an American and now owned by the National Trust, Hidcote features a series of small gardens, each given over to a theme or kind of flower.

⑤ The attractive gardens at Kiftsgate Court are renowned for their collection of roses and unusual trees and flowers, and command superb views over the countryside.

⑥ William Morris is said to have discovered Broadway, a village of corn-coloured stone whose 'broad way' is lined with red chestnut trees. Charles I and Cromwell used the 17th-century Lygon Arms.

⑦ An isolated little hill village, Snowshill's history goes back 1,000 years. Snowshill Manor House (NT) dates back to around 1500 and has a lovely terraced garden and a collection of toys, clocks and musical instruments.

⑧ At over 1,000ft, the views from the 18th-century Broadway Tower are magnificent. Other attractions are an adventure playground and a collection of rare animals and birds.

⑨ A former centre of the wool industry, Chipping Campden has an impressive 15th-century 'wool' church and a fine Jacobean market hall. Traditional crafts are kept alive at the pottery and the Campden Weavers.

⑩ Blockley's 19th-century silk-throwing mills harmonise well with contemporary cottages and add character to this attractive village.

⑪ With its steep cottage-lined street leading to a lovely old church, Bourton-on-the-Hill is an artist's delight. St Lawrence's holds many treasures, the Winchester Bushel and Peck being of special interest.

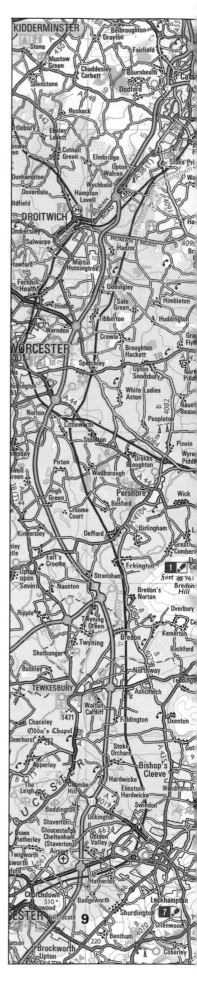

TOUR 2
TOWNS AND VILLAGES OF THE CENTRAL COTSWOLDS

Predominantly upon quiet roads this switchback drive links the Evenlode, Windrush, Leach and Coln valleys, delving to the heart of Cotswold country.

ROUTE DIRECTIONS

The drive starts from Chipping Norton. 71 miles.

Leave the Market Place on the A361①. After 5 miles descend into Shipton-under-Wychwood from where it climbs out of the Evenlode valley and into the Windrush valley to Fulbrook and Burford.

Cross the ancient narrow bridge, ascend Burford's steep High Street to the A40 roundabout, go straight over following signs to the Cotswold Wildlife Park②. Passing by the hamlet of Signet, after 2 miles turn right, unclassified road, pass the entrance to the Wildlife Park and after ½ mile go right into Holwell. Pass through Holwell and, after ¾ mile, Westwell, continuing along unclassified road signed Eastleach. After 2½ miles the road slips through the Leach valley; bear right③ and in a further 2¼ miles reach Hatherop. Turn right passing entrance to Williamstrip Park into Coln St Aldwyns, turn right opposite Coln Stores, then left, signed Bibury④.

Joining the B4425 go left, then branch right beside the Swan Hotel, unclassified road, passing the trout farm. Bear left through Ablington, signed Fossebridge, then right signed Winson. After 1 mile, turn right signed 'Village Only' passing Winson's Norman church, advancing beside the Coln meadows through Coln Rogers to Coln St Dennis. Go right at the church, then left, signed Northleach. The broad verged byway leads 3 miles north, across at Salt Way⑤, to enter Northleach Market Square.

Go left along the High Street, turning right, A429, Fosse Way, passing the Countryside Collection⑥, and as the hill steepens turn left, unclassified road, signed Hampnett. Pass through the village via gates to cross the A40, bearing right signed Turkdean. Dip into Lower

Dean bearing right at The Snicket, then beyond Dean House, turn sharp left to Upper Dean. In 1½ miles enter, right, the estate village of Notgrove, bear right signed Cold Aston, then left, signed Bourton. Go straight over the A436, bearing right following the unenclosed unclassified road down to Lower Harford (ford). Cross the B4068 to Naunton rising to the junction with B4068 and subsequent crossroads, turn right, unclassified road, signed Guiting Power. Retain the valley road via Barton, Kineton, Temple Guiting and Ford, then cross B4077. After ¼ mile bear right at the crossroads signed Cutsdean, rising on to Cutsdean Hill⑦.

Go right following Buckle Street via the Trafalgar Woods crossroads, the Cotswold Farm Park⑧, Huntsman's Quarries and across the B4068 to reach Bourton Bridge. Turn left after a short distance along the Fosse Way and turn right after Slaughter Pike garage, signed Wyck Rissington⑨. Cross former railway to enter village and continue up the steep road to Wyck Beacon tumulus, turning right, then left at the crossroads beside RAF Little Rissington.

Go right, A424, taking first turn left into Church Westcote. Turn right passing the common with its view across the Evenlode valley and soon enter Idbury. Turn right, then left signed Fifield; ¾ mile beyond Fifield, at a staggered crossroads go left signed Bruern. Pass Bruern Abbey School and go over the level crossing rising beside Lineham Golf Course to a T-junction. Go left signed Churchill and after ⅓ mile turn right signed Sarsden. At the Butter Cross go left, dipping and rising into Churchill⑩; here turn right, B4450, to return to Chipping Norton.

POINTS OF INTEREST

① The ridgetop road reveals excellent views eastwards to Wychwood Forest (*see* Walk 13) and beyond the Lyneham long barrow megalith westwards over the beautiful Evenlode vale to Stow-on-the-Wold.

② Animals and birds from all over the world can be seen in the Cotswold Wildlife Park, a large area of lake-watered wooded parkland.

③ As the Hatherop road levels on leaving the Leach valley, notice the course of Akeman Street, the 'Roman road to Bath', remarkably preserved in the pasture bank below.

④ The Coln-side scene in Bibury includes Arlington Row, a group of 17th-century weavers' cottages and Arlington Mill, a working mill and folk museum.

⑤ The principal trade route for medieval salt carriers between the saltpans at Droitwich and London, via Thames barges from Lechlade.

⑥ The story of everyday rural life in the Cotswolds is told in the Cotswold Countryside Collection, once a 'country prison'.

⑦ By logical deduction, if Cutsdean derives from the Saxon family-name Code's valley, then Cutsdean Hill was the original Code's wold, from which has come Cotswold.

⑧ Cotswold sheep, Old Gloucester cows and many other rare breeds of farm animals are on show at the Cotswold Farm Park.

⑨ Wyck Rissington church can boast having had the composer Gustav Holst as organist.

⑩ Birthplace of two notable 18th-century figures; Warren Hastings, the first Governor General of Bengal and William Smith, canal engineer and 'Father of British Geology' (*see* rugged memorial).

TOUR 3
THE INFANT THAMES

From Cirencester, the route follows the Thames from its reputed source, through Ewen and Ashton Keynes to its confluence with the Coln and the Leach at Lechlade, passing pretty villages on the way.

ROUTE DIRECTIONS

The drive starts from Cirencester ①.
67 miles.

From Cirencester follow the signs The South West and Chippenham to leave by the A429. In 1½ miles go forward, A433, signed Bristol. After another mile, in the meadows to the right, beyond the turning for Coates, is the reputed source of the River Thames. Pass under a railway bridge and turn left, unclassified road for Kemble. Cross the main road into the village, then go over the staggered crossroads, signed Ewen. The infant Thames is first seen before reaching Ewen.

Continue with the South Cerney signs and keep forward at all crossroads to reach South Cerney②.

In South Cerney turn right at the war memorial into Broadway Lane, and in ¾ mile pass, on the right, the Cotswold Marina. This is part of the Cotswold Water Park③.

Half a mile farther, at the crossroads, turn right, B4696, signed Ashton Keynes. In 1¼ miles turn left and shortly branch left, unclassified road, to reach Ashton Keynes. The stripling Thames, only a few feet wide, flows through the village.

At the end of the village turn left on to the Cricklade road then bear right. Two miles farther, at the crossroads, turn left, B4040, and after another 1½ miles turn left again to enter Cricklade. Turn right along Calcutt Street following signs Swindon, then in ¾ mile join the A419. One mile farther turn left for Castle Eaton. Continue on the Highworth road to pass through Hannington. In 1¼ miles turn left, B4019, for Highworth④.

Turn left on to the Stow road, A361. After 4½ miles, on the left, a riverside park is passed before crossing the old Halfpenny Bridge into Lechlade⑤.

Turn right, then right again to leave by the A417, and in ¾ mile cross St John's Bridge⑥.

Two miles farther the drive passes the grounds of Buscot House⑦.

Keep straight ahead to Faringdon. From the Market Square branch left on to the A4095, and after passing the church turn left. In 2½ miles cross Radcot Bridge⑧.

At Clanfield the drive goes forward, B4020, for Alvescot. In ¼ mile turn left, unclassified road, to Kencot, and in 1¼ miles at the crossroads turn right into Filkins⑨.

In the village turn right and in 1 mile, at the T-junction, turn right, A361, signed Stow. In 2 miles at the crossroads turn left, unclassified road, signed Wildlife Park, and pass the entrance to the Cotswold Wildlife Park⑩.

In ½ mile go over the crossroads, signed Eastleach Martin, then after ½ mile, branch left and follow a narrow by-road to the twin Eastleaches. At Eastleach Martin cross the River Leach into Eastleach Turville, then keep right through the village on the Hatherop road. In ½ mile, at the T-junction, turn left, then in ½ mile turn right, and 2 miles farther turn right again into Hatherop. Turn left for Coln St Aldwyns⑪.

Turn left, signed Fairford, then cross the River Coln and ascend into Quenington. At the green turn left, then at the end of the village recross the Coln and continue to Fairford⑫.

The drive returns to Cirencester on the A417 through the villages of Poulton and Ampney Crucis.

POINTS OF INTEREST

① The Roman capital of the Cotswolds, Cirencester is a pleasant market town with a Norman abbey gateway and a 15th-century 'wool' church. Cirencester Park is open to the public.

② Around 4,000 acres of lakes will have been created from gravel pits around South Cerney. The village itself retains its Cotswold heart and has three manors.

③ The Water Park – a series of 100 man-made lakes – attracts human and wildfowl visitors alike.

④ Highworth is a hill-top town with some 17th-century houses and a 15th-century church.

⑤ The rivers Coln and Leach join the Thames at Lechlade. Shelley composed his *Summer Evening Meditation* in Lechlade churchyard during 1815.

⑥ An Augustinian hospital gave its name to the 13th-century St John's Bridge, the street leading to it and to St John's Lock, beyond which large boats cannot navigate the Thames.

⑦ Built in the Adam style in 1780, Buscot House is surrounded by landscaped gardens.

⑧ The 14th-century Radcot Bridge is the oldest recorded bridging point on the Upper Thames and was built by the monks of Beaulieu Abbey.

⑨ In Filkins, the Cotswold Woollen Weavers keep old skills alive in an 18th-century barn, and there is a small museum and an old village lock-up.

⑩ Set in 200 acres of lake-watered wooded parkland, the Cotswold Wildlife Park contains animals and birds from all over the world.

⑪ Sturdy stone cottages line Coln St Aldwyn's main street. Barns, cottages and a manorial farm group with the mainly Norman church are to the west; to the east is Williamstrip Park, a classical 17th-century mansion.

⑫ The magnificent stained-glass windows of the late 15th-century church at Fairford are the only complete set of their period to survive intact in the British Isles.

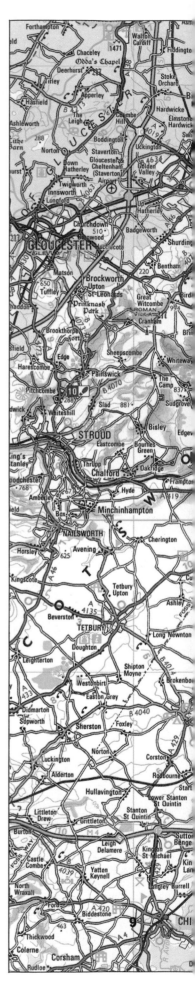

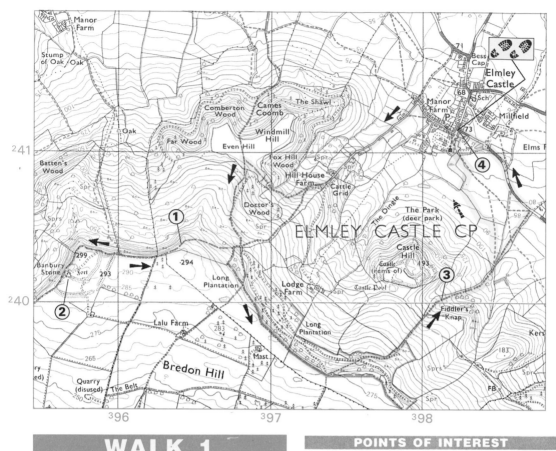

WALK 1

BREDON HILL

Bredon Hill is literally and metaphorically the high point of this walk. The climb is steep in parts, but well repays the effort for the panoramic views — to 'see the coloured counties and hear the larks so high', as A E Housman put it in a poem published in *A Shropshire Lad*.

ROUTE DIRECTIONS

Approx. 5 miles. Allow 2½ hours.
Start from the broad main street of Elmley Castle (grid ref. SO982412). Park either along the wide-verged Kersoe road or in the broad main street of Elmley Castle.
Take the road leading north-west from the Queen Elizabeth public house, passing the former post office (closed 1984) and several delightful half-timbered cottages. Bear left along the lane to Hill House Farm.

A bridleway leads up the sunken path to the gate. Stay on the main track climbing between Doctor's Wood and Fox Hill Wood to the right of two gates. Follow the fence upon Even Hill to a (frequently muddy) gate midway along the fence, here joining the bridle track on its steady ascent of the slumped scarp slope. Arriving at a gate into Long Plantation, turn sharp right up the eroded bank by the short edge of woodland, then angle right, steadily gaining height, to emerge upon the startling edge①.

Follow the scarp-top track via a gate by the pine copse, to accompany the wall to Parson's Folly②.

Retrace your steps, keeping to the wire fence and skirting the top of Long Plantation, until the Wychavon District Council sign to their 'Way' (yellow crown) directs you left down through the scarp woodland and rough pastures by two hunting gates③.

At the second blue bridle gate, either take the short cut on a modified footpath via stiles along the boundary of the park (white waymarks) making entry into the village through the churchyard, or continue down to the Kersoe road to re-enter via the 'hole in the wall'④.

POINTS OF INTEREST

① Northward views open up from this excellent scarpland prospect, extending in clear weather as far as The Wrekin, and the Clent and Lickey Hills, south of Birmingham.

② Parson's Folly was erected during the late 18th century by the owner of Kemerton Court, with the intention of setting the viewing platform at 1,000ft. Unfortunately, the tower now houses telecommunications apparatus. Nevertheless, the panorama is, without question, stunning — with the patchwork of fields, orchards and woodlands spreading across the vale. The hillscape includes the Cotswold edge south-east from Meon Hill to Coopers Hill, the Forest of Dean, with the Monnow Hills south-west across the Severn, and the Malverns to the west. The summit of Bredon is hemmed in by double ramparts of Kemerton Camp, an Iron Age hill fort on the south and east. The Banbury Stone, in the cleft below the prospect tower, was created by the bonding of calcite solution and partially crumbled limestone bedrock. It was believed to have been used ceremonially during the Iron Age occupation of the hill-fort.

③ Away to the left are the massive bracken-covered earthworks of Beauchamp Castle, once held by descendants of the Earls of Warwick. It was built by Robert le Despenser in the late 11th century and became for a time the principal seat of the Beauchamps. Following a period of neglect, the castle was re-fortified in the 14th century, only to be once more in decay by the early 16th century.

④ Allow time after the walk to explore Elmley Castle, a quintessential English village where children dance round the maypole on Oak Apple Day (29 May). Take the opportunity of inspecting the parish church before you leave for it contains a model and detailed history of Beauchamp Castle and dynasty together with several interesting memorials, notably that of the Earls of Coventry from Croome Court near Pershore, who were responsible for building Broadway Tower.

WALK 2

DOVER'S HILL

The Cotswold Edge at Dover's Hill is the setting for this short walk, which gives memorable views northwards over the Vale of Evesham. The walk can conveniently be extended (more than doubling the length) to visit the medieval wool centre of Chipping Campden, seen at its best from an off-the-hill pedestrian approach. Stout shoes or wellingtons are advisable in wet weather within Lynches Wood.

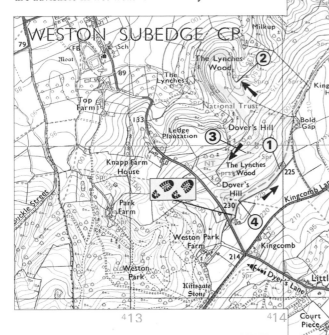

ROUTE DIRECTIONS

Approx. 1¾ miles. Allow 1 hour.
Start from the Dover's Hill National Trust car park (grid ref. SP136395).

Go through the adapted kissing-gate and follow the escarpment edge ahead①. At Bold Gap the path descends towards a wooden squeeze stile. Do not cross this stile; instead, descend the pasture, passing a waymark post, and enter the wood at the stile next to the gate (not the Weston path stile).

The Ordnance Survey map shows none of the paths within Lynches Wood② so be guided by the National Trust waymark posts along the main track rounding the spur. After crossing a heavily used bridle path, the path loses height before turning sharp left③. The walk rises beside the terraces, until guided left again to a flight of earthen steps and bears right at the top to leave the wood via the stile.

Advance to join a cart track, following the fence up the pasture, and keep to the right. At the scrub-surrounded spring leave the track left, making a diagonal ascent to the prominent ridge and completing the ascent within a shallow hollow way to the topograph④.

To extend the walk from this location follow the Cotswold Way waymarks to Kingcomb Lane, then down Hoo Lane to explore Chipping Campden⑤. Stroll along the curving High Street to the church, returning by Sheep Street, Westington, Blind and Dyer's lanes.

POINTS OF INTEREST

① The extensive westward views from the scarp feature Dumbleton and Bredon hills backed by the Malvern range; below spreads the green fertile Vale of Evesham.

② Lynches Wood refers to the terraced north-west facing bank, within the wood. Here lie a series of medieval cultivation strips created when pressure for ploughland was acute.

③ The Lynches Wood strips are contemporary with the ridge and furrow fossilised within the open pasture leading up to the Dover's Hill scarp, an affirmation of the demand for arable land from the Manor of Weston-sub-Edge. It is thought that these strip lynchets were often used during the Romano-British period for vineyards. Indeed, directly below the woodland fruit orchards still exist.

④ Resembling a garden sundial stand, the elegant 'topograph' commemorates the efforts of F L Griggs to acquire this estate for public enjoyment in the 1920s. The splendid natural amphitheatre of Dover's Hill, now protected by the National Trust, is the venue, every summer, for the 'Cotswold Olympicks' — Robert Dover's Games. Founded in 1612, the Games include rural sports such as tug-of-war, greasy pole and shin kicking, together with dancing and other entertainment; it is now linked with the Scuttlebrook Wake Fair.

⑤ Chipping Campden could scarcely have a more appropriate motto than 'History in Stone'. The glow of golden Cotswold limestone is everywhere, in such High Street buildings as the Jacobean Market Hall, and the Woolstaplers' Hall (housing the museum), but pride of place goes to the almshouses leading to St James's — one of the finest Cotswold 'wool' churches.

WALK 3

STANTON AND STANWAY

High, scenic ridge tracks, lush pastureland paths and two classic honey-toned stone villages typifies the true essence of the Cotswolds.

ROUTE DIRECTIONS

Approx. 4¾ miles. Allow 2¼ hours.
Park in the visitor car park adjacent to the village hall and cricket ground at Stanton (grid ref. SP067344).
Follow the road right passing Stanton Court and bear left into the main street①. At the head of the street fork right, via Little Sheppey, directed by Cotswold Way waymarks along the gated track. Prior to the third gate bear right to a stiled passage between water tanks and a pond. Climb the bank directly ahead, keep to the right of the jumps and angle across the shallow valley before rising to a stile on the right. Follow the stream uphill, by a hydraulic ram, to reach the stile on the left into the narrow upper dry valley. Ascend to the gate on the lip of Shenberrow Camp, to the left of Shenberrow Buildings.

Traverse the camp plateau, then, leaving the Cotswold Way, go right to the grid and gate, and swing round passing through the farmyard. At the bridleway sign pass through the gate, heading south-west, with the wall to the right, via two further gates.

Bear right upon the footpath above the combe to the stile and join the track running south-east beside the wall and along the top of Lidcombe Wood. At the end of the wood and track junction, go right towards Parks Farm.

Descend through the gate below the buildings, waymarked with green topped posts, leading directly into the woodland glade. Watch for the 'bridleway this direction' sign at the foot of the valley, guiding left. Ascend the track beside a wall, overlooking Papermill Farm. A path completes the descent to the foot of

Oldhill and on to the pavement alongside the Stanway Hill road (B4077).

Follow the pavement for ¼ mile to rejoin the Cotswold Way right, at the stile where the broad avenue meets the road. Descend the green way to a kissing-gate to join the minor road leading through the village passing Stanway House② and winding past the church③. The Cotswold Way to Stanton is meticulously waymarked from the stile off the road right. A second fence stile leads to a crossing of the parkland avenue to another stile. From the succeeding gate, a series of stiles advance the footpath over pastureland④ to a short lane that leads back into the village of Stanton; conclude the walk by passing Manorway, the original Tudor manor.

POINTS OF INTEREST

① Stanton's picturesque cohesion derives as much from its proximity to a generous source of the very best honey-toned Cotswold building stone and the sensitive development of several centuries, as to Sir Philip Stott's sympathetic restorations during the first third of the present century.

② Stanway House, home of the Earl of Wemyss, is an exemplary example of Jacobean style. It was built between 1580 and 1640 on the site of an abbey by the Tracys, a local landowning family. Its interest lies in its development as a typical squire's manor house. The elaborate gatehouse, thought to be the work of Timothy Strong of Barrington, was built about 1630 and is adorned with scallop shells, the family crest of the Tracys.

③ The tithe barn dates from the 14th century when the manor belonged to Tewkesbury Abbey. The cricket pavilion perched on staddlestones was built by Sir James Barrie, architect of the Palace of Westminster.

④ The ridge and furrow, a characteristic feature of the Lias clay pastures below the Cotswold escarpment, is being overcome by landslipping, as though it were a lava flow.

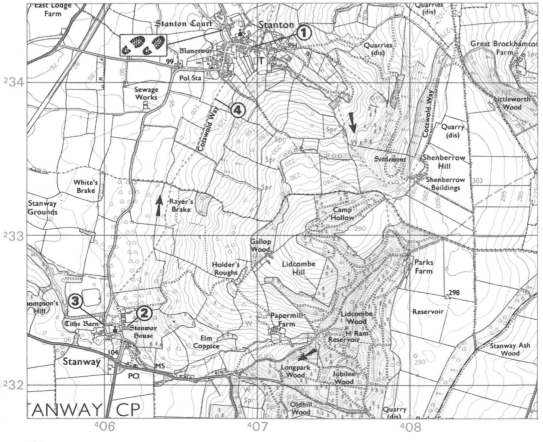

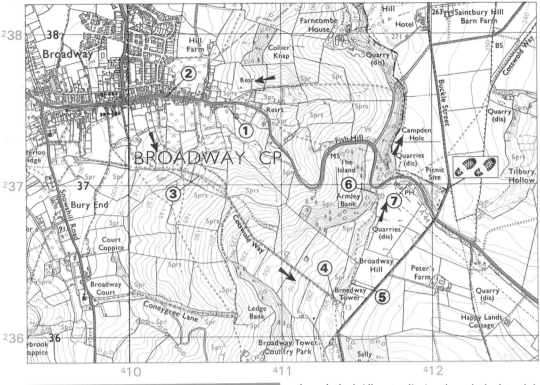

WALK 4

TOWERING OVER BROADWAY

Broadway has emerged as one of the most popular village attractions in the Cotswolds. Yet despite its geographical location, beneath an almost exclusively Gloucestershire Cotswold scarp, a quirk of history rendered the hill pastures being included (and still remaining) in Worcestershire. (For prior to Henry VIII's Dissolution of the monasteries the manor was held by the abbot of Pershore Abbey.) The approach to Broadway Tower is a sustained climb and may well be considered strenuous.

ROUTE DIRECTIONS

Approx. 5 miles. Allow 2¼ hours.
Start from the Fish Hill picnic site (grid ref. SP120369).
Follow the 'Woodland Walk' signs, rising to the Donald Russell Memorial 'topograph' (denied a real prospect by the scarp beechwood). Passing the Cotswold Way sign, descend into an old quarry on a clearly waymarked path (red-topped posts) via steps. Emerging at the far end, contour right through the Campden Hole beechwood; in due course the path descends to a stile, crosses the road by the entrance to Farncombe House to a stile, signed 'Broadway'.

Descend straight down the pasture to a stile, then continuing on the pasture way join the hardcore track beside a hedge leading eventually to a handgate. Follow the iron railing to a stile on to the main road next to Pike Cottage.

Walkers may like to stroll down the street① & ② to window-gaze before backtracking to the point where the Cotswold Way leaves the street on its long ascent to Broadway Tower③. Branch left at Peartree House along a short lane crossing two stiles to enter a small pasture. The footpath slants left via stiles and up old ridge and furrow. Steadily gaining height in the slumped pasture, keep alongside the wall via stone flag stiles latterly beside open farmland, to enter the Broadway Tower Country Park over a new stile④.

Rising directly to the foot of the Tower, go left through the bridle gate slipping through the lateral dry valley⑤. Continue on the Cotswold Way to a gate into woodland⑥. Keeping straight ahead, carefully cross the A44 on the sweeping curve below the Fish Inn to finish the walk⑦.

POINTS OF INTEREST

① The houses in upper Broadway are very grand, Top and Orchard Farms being far removed from the traditional Cotswold farmhouse. Down the 'broad way' notice the Lygon Arms Hotel and the harmonious blend of cottage styles.

② The spacious, tree-lined main street makes it easy to see how Broadway got its name—though the original 'broad way' was probably the present Snowshill Road, where both Broadway Court and the old parish church, St Eadburgh's, are situated. This church dedication derives from a patron saint of Pershore Abbey, the Abbots of which had their summer grange here. Evidence of this can be found along the new 'broad way' in the Prior's Manse, by the junction of Leamington Road and Abbot's Grange situated just below the green; both are dated circa 1320.

③ Ahead is Broadway Tower, built on a beacon site in 1798 at the whim of the Countess of Coventry, wife of the sixth Earl, who lived at Croome Court and nearby Spring Hill House. Designed by James Wyatt the 65ft tower, set at 1,024ft, is one of the finest panoramic viewpoints in lowland England.

④ Nature trails, an adventure playground and a collection of farm animals are among the outdoor attractions of the Broadway Tower Country Park, while the tower itself houses exhibitions on three floors, and an observation room with a telescope, giving wonderful views over 12 counties.

⑤ This scrub filled dry valley was formed as a slip trough from the downward movement of fractured limestone bedrock on the unstable clay bed beneath the initial scarp face.

⑥ 'Armley' is derived from the Saxon word for 'wretched', so Armley Bank may have been a refuge for beggars and outlaws.

⑦ Originally a summer-house for Farncombe House, the quaint Fish Inn later became an ale-house catering for weary travellers at the crest of Fish Hill.

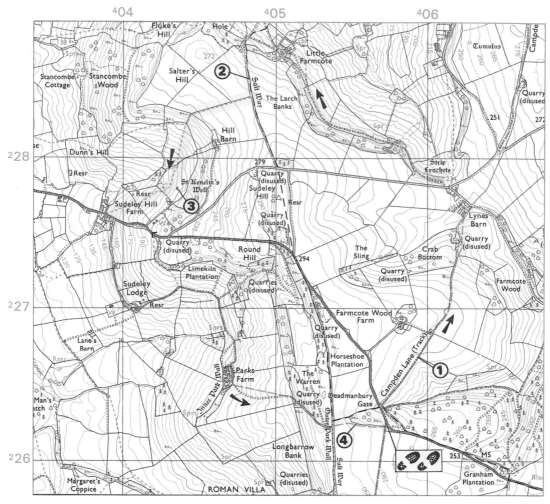

WALK 5

SALTER'S HILL

A scenic, undulating ramble along established tracks and designated 'Ways', affording panoramic views across to Bredon Hill and the Vale of Evesham.

ROUTE DIRECTIONS

Approx. 5 miles. Allow 2½ hours.
Car parking is available at Deadmanbury Gate (grid ref. SP057262)

Follow the road north, branching right 10yds beyond the Warden's Way footpath sign. Join the bridleway which opens on to the Campden Lane track①. Shortly after passing a derelict cottage, the track begins to descend, superceding an overgrown holloway to a gate, then follows the fence past an old quarry down to a gate on to the unclassified road adjacent to Lynes Barn. Go left, and left again at the junction, entering the pasture at the first gate on the right. Follow the track bearing left and contour along a medieval cultivation terrace, past a barn to a temporary gate. The path continues left through the copse via gates, crossing an old droveway to a gateway. Continue contouring the pasture beneath Larch Banks to the gate, descend half-right towards the fenced enclosure. Pass below the large portal-framed cattle shed, rising left via gates through the farmyard of Little Farmcote. From the cattle grid the track forks; bear left to the unenclosed Salter's Lane road②, and go left, uphill (not on the new cut private access).

Leave the Salt Way at a footpath sign, turning right on the north side of a wall crossing the Salter's Hill ridge and then descending to a gate. Entering the pastures at the head of Stancombe, descend to a redundant gate. Descend directly south towards the obvious track and from a second gate follow the track, briefly diverting to inspect St Kenelm's Well③. Leave the track immediately after the gate below the farmhouse and gently descend to another gate, continuing half-right to a gate on to the road beside Sudeley Hill Farm.

Go left, then right above the farm buildings, along the road signed 'Sudeley Lodge and Parks Farm'. Pass through Sudeley Lodge courtyard, keeping left, and proceed via gates uphill by the grain store, rising upon the road, which levels as it curves round the combe, before rising again to pass close above Parks Farm. Follow the track directly east, ascending through the beech shelter-belt, on to the ridge road by the rough pasture of Longbarrow Bank. Go left, then right④, following the waymarked route to finish.

POINTS OF INTEREST

① Campden Lane has ancient roots complying with the natural Cotswold ridgeway, its name deriving from its medieval function as a drove route to the wool market at Chipping Campden.

② Though there must have been numerous splinter routes serving manors far and wide, this is the principal Salters' trade route linking Droitwich with London via Lechlade and the Thames.

③ St Kenelm's Well, marked by a conduit house, was built in 1887 by Lord Chandos of Sudeley Castle to coincide with the visit of Queen Victoria. In origin this shrine was contrived and cultivated by the abbot of St Peter's Abbey in Winchcombe to attract pilgrims. Kenelm, the boy-king of Mercia, son of Kenwulf, was buried alongside his father at Winchcombe in AD 819.

④ The Warden's Way (13 miles) links Winchcombe with Bourton-on-the-Water via a string of villages, thus forming a union of the Cotswold–Wychavon and Oxfordshire Ways.

▲ Native stone edges a low footbridge over Hilcot Brook as the walk wends between steeply wooded banks near Pinchley Wood.

WALK 6

COLD COMFORT COMMON

Although quite close to Cheltenham, at the foot of the Cotswold escarpment, this is a high wold walk in an area which has a surprisingly remote feel to it. Stretches of woodland around the route shelter songbirds and small mammals, and there are fine views to savour.

ROUTE DIRECTIONS

Approx. 4 miles. Allow 1¾ hours.
Start from the Kilkenny Viewpoint car park (grid ref. SP004186).
Walk up the Hilcot road, passing the mast and larch clump①. Branch left from the road immediately prior to entering into a belt of beeches. Cross the stile beside the trap jump to reach the fence stile at the wall corner. Keep strictly to the footpath through the tiny reservoir enclosure via stiles②.

Progress to join a track leading over Withington Hill, latterly alongside a fence to a gate. Go immediately right through the gate and follow the track leading down beside Smoke Acre③.

The track passes through a new gate (beneath the word 'Acre' on the map), and continues under power-lines, a striking (though unwelcome) addition to this landscape. Leave the track (landowner modified route) where it swings right, crossing the stile. Advance beside the fence to reach a stile on the left, and descend the steep bank, harbouring ancient herbage, to a handgate at the foot of a dry valley. A lane crosses the Hilcot Brook with its pretty pond and rises via a gate to the minor road. Go right here passing the attractive Upper Hilcot Farm.

The walk follows the road initially beside Hilcot Brook, sheltered by wooded banks④, then rises by Rough Hill Bank to regain the unenclosed road to return to Cold Comfort Common.

POINTS OF INTEREST

① St Paul's Epistle, a hilltop tumulus garnished by wind-battered larches, derives its curious name from the practice of reciting passages from the Bible at significant high points during the old custom of reasserting the parish limits known as 'beating the bounds'. The 948ft hill is a good viewpoint: the panorama stretches across the Severn Vale to the Malverns in the north-west, and in the opposite direction to the Thamesdown Hills above Swindon.

② The route accompanies the ridge wall with wide, pleasing views over Foxcote and the upper Coln valley, a river that rises just a few hundred yards east of the footpath.

③ The name of Smoke Acre is thought to be derived from the medieval practice of paying for rented land with 'smoke pennies' in place of tithewood.

④ Pinchley Wood derives its name from the Old English word 'pinc' meaning finch. The steep slope to the west is appropriately known as Breakneck Bank, while Ratshill Bank, farther along speaks for itself — though you are more likely to spot the furtive tree-rat (grey squirrel) as you rise out of this beautifully wooded dell.

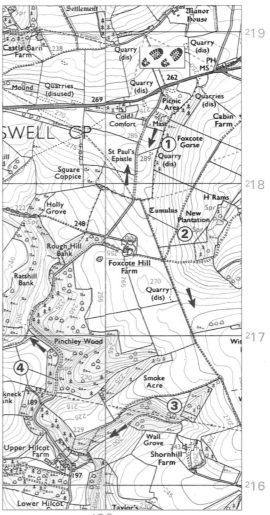

WALK 7

DEVIL'S CHIMNEY

An invigorating, simple-to-follow walk on firm ground with superb scarp and wold views, intriguing quarries, a pretty village with notable connections and the 'real' source of the Thames are all encountered on this walk.

ROUTE DIRECTIONS

Approx. 6 miles. Allow 3 hours.
Start at the Seven Springs lay-by (grid ref. SO966169).
① Walk north-east to the staggered cross-roads of the A436 with the A435, turn left and left again along the minor road accompanying the Cotswold Way (waymarking distinguished by a white dot).

Where the road swings sharp left continue forward within the bridle lane, watching for the sharp break left, up and around the field and alongside the wall rising through bracken on to Charlton Kings Common. This promenade is notable for its far ranging views over Cheltenham and the Severn Vale to the Malvern Hills. The path crosses the Iron Age hill-fort to a sign directing right for the Devil's Chimney②.

Return to the edge path running south over the short turf, passing old quarry incursions and Salterley Grange Quarry. Descend to the road, then turn left uphill till a signpost to Ullenwood directs right, down the bridle track, which shortly becomes a fenced lane adjacent to the golf course.

Meeting the road go left, leaving the Cotswold Way, and follow the road past the club house and up to the junction with the A436. Cross directly over on to the

Cowley road, branching immediately right through the double gates on to the unenclosed track rising on to South Hill.

At the brow of the hill bear left along the ridgetop passing Cuckoopen Barn③. The track descends the ridge via gates passing a long barrow above Coldwell Bottom. Upon reaching the minor road follow this eastwards to where a bridle lane branches off left beside the wall passing Close Farm. Cross the stile beside a gate, descending the pasture to a stile and footbridge climbing to a kissing-gate. Join the road here making a diversion to Coberley Court, wherein hides St Giles's Church④.

Either go directly up the path ahead to the cross or, if you have opted to visit St Giles's, follow the street forking right up to the tiny primary school. Continue along the trackway beyond the council houses, branching right at a stile along a narrow fenced footpath back to Seven Springs.

POINTS OF INTEREST

① Seven Springs form the highest tributary risings of the River Thames and are the most distant from London. The River Churn, flowing south through Cirencester, meets the Thames near Cricklade.

② Devil's Chimney well merits the brief detour to inspect its slender pinnacle. Created about 1780 by quarrymen (initially by accident it is thought) it was quickly recognised as a good marketing ploy and further sculpted in order to draw attention to their activities as a source of quality building stone.

③ Notice the silver plaque by the barn proclaiming 'the World's Biggest Straw Rick' — 40,400 bales, achieved in 1982.

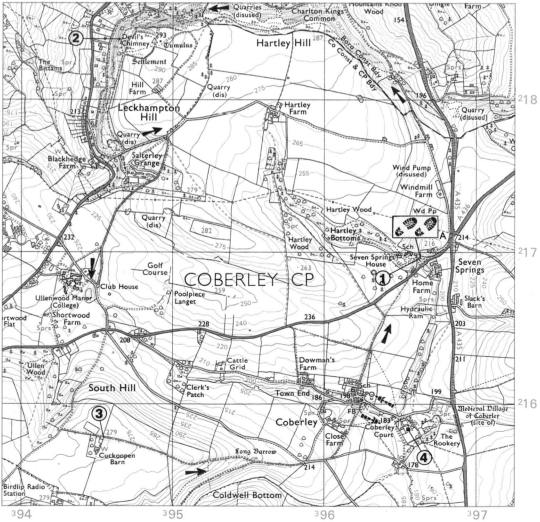

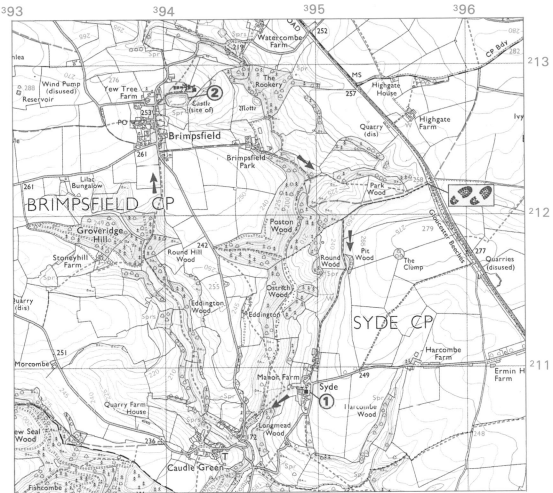

④ St Giles's Church, approached through a barn-door and 'private' garden, was originally built as a chantry for the Berkeley family in 1340. Their monuments adorn the church, and include the mother of the famed Dick Whittington, thrice Lord Mayor of London.

WALK 8

BRIMPSFIELD

The A417T realignment which created the long Gloucester Beeches lay-by, with toilet block and frequent snack caravan makes the perfect launch pad for a walk into the beautifully secluded head-stream combes of the River Frome.

ROUTE DIRECTIONS

Approx. 4¾ miles. Allow 2 hours.
Park at Gloucester Beeches (grid ref. SO958123).
Cross successive stiles at the northern end of the plantation and follow the fence beside the wall leading south-west. Reaching a stile enter a lane wending south to the tiny village of Syde①. At the road junction follow the upper road for 100yds, then bear right to enter the churchyard. Continue through, beyond the porch, to the narrow passage on to the roadway. Go left, then right (footpath sign) through a gated yard (this can be muddy). Descend by the pond and old sheep dip, bearing left via the steep pasture on a shelf path to the gate between two mature redwood trees. Cross the subsequent stile and follow the drive past the secluded cottage to reach the road junction below Fernhill Cottages (lane to Keepers Cottage right). Cross the facing wall stile climbing the steep bank to a second wall stile and turn right into Caudle Green.

Enter the mid-hamlet green attractively surrounded by cottages, and passing the bus stop bear right, before a farmhouse, at the footpath sign, then descend through the cleared thicket via stiles. Crossing the stream, turn left through the hunting gate, follow the valley floor footpath winding north. Where the valley divides, bear right to reach the stile, then hold left keeping the woodland to the left. Rise out of the valley on a green way via gates on to the Brimpsfield road.

Walk straight through the village and take the footpath right, signposted 'to the church'. This is a pleasant, optional, spur route, providing an intimate view of the castle earthworks②. The main route, however, continues across the pasture to the stile and gently down the ensuing pasture to a stile on to the narrow unclassified road. Go right, downhill, almost into the valley bottom, follow the lane branching right above Ivy Cottage signed 'Common Cottage' and just beyond Common Cottage pass through a wicket gate, descending steps to follow the clearly waymarked path beside the stream through the woodland to a stile. Go left along the track rising into a pasture with a view of 17th-century Brimpsfield Park. Proceed via two stiles, descending to cross plank footbridges between the two ponds. Joining the bridle track go left and at the gate leave the valley by following the track rising ahead. Sweeping up to a gate, the bridle track accompanies the wall via two further gates to complete the walk.

POINTS OF INTEREST

① The tiny village of Syde rests exquisitely upon a brink overlooking the upper Frome valley, with Tudor manor house, tithe barn and saddleback-towered Early Norman church.

② Brimpsfield castle mound was erected in succession to the small motte in the valley below by Walter Giffard. Built substantially with inner keep and bailey it was slighted following the family's part in a rebellion against Edward II, many stones finding their way into the charming little church standing adjacent and remote from the village.

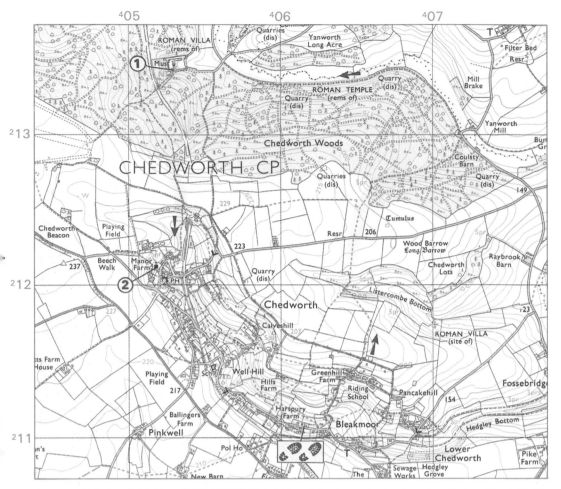

WALK 9
CHEDWORTH WOODS

A splendid marriage of village, woodland and valley ways, a rural ribbon drawn together around a quiet tree-shaded passage of the River Coln. Tucked within an embowered combe is the most perfect Roman villa, a scene that can have altered little in eighteen hundred years. The walk crosses open farmland and treads woodland paths that can be muddy in wet weather.

ROUTE DIRECTIONS

Approx. 5 miles. Allow 2¼ hours.
Start near Hartpury Farm where the street broadens in the middle of Chedworth (grid ref. SP162111).
Follow the village street east and directly after Saffron Hill bear left via a low stile to enter, and descend, Green Lane. Dipping through the valley, ascend through Greenhill Farm, proceeding straight over the bridle-lane, and following the estate footpath sign into the narrow enclosure. Beyond a gate a County Council footpath sign directs walkers left over the wall; proceed north-west to a simple fence stile. Cross the finger of farmland on the same line to a further simple fence stile continuing through the woodland directly into Listercombe Bottom. Follow the tractor track climbing straight up the opposing bank, switching right through the thicket at the top to enter a field. Go due north crossing a minor road (footpath signs), progress through the enlarged (walls removed) field making for the two sycamore trees, and then bear right to the broad grass headland descending to the gateway (footpath sign) into Chedworth Woods. The valley track descends towards Coulsty Barn, but the footpath veers

left where a track enters abruptly from the right. Slip over the woodland ridge to a simple stile next to the cottage at Yanworth Mill, then follow the private drive north, signed Roman villa 1½ miles.

Reaching the crossroads go left up the lane to the Roman villa and continue on the footpath beyond the Interpretive Centre①, beneath the old railway, turning left at the cross paths. The path winds up to a stile exiting the woods, rising to successive stiles beside the fence, and over the ridge to a gate. Go forward to a stile and follow steps down the wooded bank to a further stile. Cross the valley pasture keeping right to a stile into the village lane. Proceed beyond the church②, down the narrow path to The Seven Tuns, and through the narrow passage immediately right of the premises to a stile. Cross the paddock and, via successive stiles, the old railway. Trend down right following the series of stiles along the valley floor to a lane. Go right, uphill to a stile beside a gate. Traverse the pasture bank via stiles and latterly a gate, before rising to a stile into the short passage next to Saffron Hill.

POINTS OF INTEREST

① Chedworth Roman Villa is sensitively managed and expertly interpreted by the National Trust. Discovered in 1864, subsequent excavations revealed a villa which undoubtedly belonged to a very wealthy Roman landowner. The buildings date from AD180 to AD350 and so far over 30 rooms have been uncovered. Allow yourself ample time to inspect the baths, mosaics and enduring spring shrine.

② St Andrew's Church stands at the head of this most attractive village, the cottages and farmhouses exhibit characteristic Cotswold style and range south-eastwards for a mile and a half on either flank of this sheltered tributary combe of the Coln. The church is thought to be built on Saxon foundations, though the core is 12th century.

▲ An unequalled collection of Renaissance-style table tombs in Painswick churchyard.

WALK 10

PROSPECT OVER PARADISE

This walk enjoys the liberty of Painswick Hill and particularly the prospect from the Beacon Camp across the Severn Vale to the Forest of Dean, May Hill and the Malverns, as well as the nearby wooded scarplands. It returns in complete contrast deep within the Painswick Stream valley, concluding via Painswick's famous churchyard. The walk entails fording a small stream.

ROUTE DIRECTIONS

Approx. 5½ miles. Allow 3 hours.
Start from the free car park off Stamages Lane (grid ref. SO865095).
Walk up the pavement beside the main through road passing the lych-gate, along New Road① past the post office and at the crossroads go left up Gloucester Street, passing the Gyde Almshouses. Now accompanying the Cotswold Way (white dot added to conventional waymark arrows), bear right up the minor road leading on to the common. Branch left opposite the reservoir gates, but do not follow the obvious track beside the plantation; instead go across the lower golf course fairway and the unenclosed road. Keeping above the cemetery, soon enter a woodland path, passing Catsbrain Quarry.

At the upper cross-ridge unenclosed road the Cotswold Way is waymarked along a contouring bridleway keeping east of Painswick Beacon; ignore this and climb directly on to the high ramparts to admire the view②.

Descend north-east on to a track above Pope's Wood, joining the metalled lane leading down to the Royal William Hotel. Turn left to the bus stop, then leave the Cotswold Way by crossing the A46, descending a bridleway on to the minor road. Continue downhill, forking right, signed 'Sheepscombe', to reach the valley bottom.

Follow the private drive signposted Tocknell's Court beside Painswick Stream, passing the beautifully tended gardens. Climb the stile between the stream and cattle grid, proceed down the valley pasture upon a green way to a gate. The footpath ahead is well waymarked with yellow arrows to the right; pass the cottage, then slant left to the site of Oliver's Mill, ford the stream and advance via a series of stiles down the pastures to Damsell's Mill.

Cross the minor road to a stone flag stile, continue above the deeply cut stream beside a fence, via two more stiles, then turn right over the bridge. Three paths diverge at this point; follow the hedgeline left going through the double stile beside a gate. Pass a circular ruin and mill pond to the gate beside Highgrove. Follow the unenclosed metalled road into Painswick town via Vicarage Street, passing the Institute③ to enter St Mary's Street and the churchyard④.

POINTS OF INTEREST

① New Street was new in 1260 when the thoroughfare changed from Bisley Street. New Street boasts several fine classically styled houses facing the churchyard, notably Hazelbury House and the Falcon Inn.

② During the Civil War Charles I gazed over the deep valley from Kimsbury and likened the setting to 'paradise'. Though the name has stuck, one wonders if his troops would have considered it so, encamped upon the exposed hilltop; after all, the King was made comfortable in Painswick Court!

③ The Painswick Institute is home of the Gloucestershire Guild of Craftsmen's annual exhibition each August.

④ In the churchyard, famed for its yew trees, the impressive 17th- and 18th-century Renaissance-styled table tombs reveal a roll-call of the wealthy clothiers and merchants of the district.

WALK 11

COTSWOLD CRAFTSMEN

Sapperton and the Daneway represent an important focus of Cotswold industrial ambition, with both late 18th-century canal tunnelling and the early 20th-century Arts and Crafts revivalism, of Gimson and the Barnsley brothers. The walk takes a dive into the wooded Frome valley where there are some steep and muddy places, so it is advisable to wear stout boots or wellingtons.

ignoring the minor path left. Continue until a more significant track is encountered and go left, eventually descending out of the woods to Dane Lane, just above Daneway House④.

Cross the road to a stile, keep to the left of the fence and traverse to Daneway Banks (nature reserve), a precious unimproved calcareous grassland. Cross the minor road by corresponding stiles entering Siccaridge Wood (nature reserve) upon a trackway. After a while the ridge path begins to descend and where three paths diverge go sharp left, initially downhill, latterly rising to a gate out of the woodland; cross the pasture to reach Dane Lane next to The Daneway Inn⑤.

Cross the old canal bridge, taking the stile left signed

▲ The abandoned Thames and Severn canal at Sapperton.

'Canal Walk'. In due course climb above the tunnel entrance to a stile, slanting up the pasture to a stile leading into Sapperton.

Keep on the main road, past the village hall, Bell Inn and Glebe Farm, continuing to the road junction. Go right, passing the precise Ordnance Survey datum 594.88ft. Then go right again into the Broad Ride to finish the walk.

POINTS OF INTEREST

① Broad Ride extends from Sapperton Common east through Lord Bathurst's Cirencester Park — 10,000 acres of the finest surviving example in England of geometrical landscaping, where great rides meet and grand vistas appear unexpectedly.

② St Kenelm's Church belongs principally to the 14th century, although the Atkyns family of Pinbury Park made embellishments around 1730. Sir Robert Atkyns, whose monument adorns the south transept, was the author of *The Ancient and Present State of Gloucestershire*, a famous early historical treatise. Pinbury was also the home of John Masefield, created Poet Laureate in 1930.

③ The house, Upper Dorvel, with its striking topiary hedge, was formed and extended from two cottages by Ernest Barnsley around 1901.

④ Daneway House, dating from around 1250, was the home of the Hancox family continuously from 1397 to 1860. At the beginning of the present century it became the workshop and showroom of the Gimson/Barnsley woodcraft partnership.

⑤ The Daneway Inn was built for the refreshment of 'bargees' and 'leggers' who worked the long Sapperton Canal Tunnel until the Great Western Railway was built in 1911.

ROUTE DIRECTIONS

Approx. 3¾ miles. Allow 1¾ hours.
Start from the Broad Ride where you can park your car next to the road (grid ref. SO947028).
Go past the Manor Farm① and the Glebe estate, then descend the footpath, right, into Sapperton village street, opposite the school and post office (there is no shop). Turn right, then fork left down the 'no through road' to the parish church②. Continue down the passage beside the church to a handgate slanting below Upper Dorvel③. Bear right to pass through the end gate in the stock pens and then immediately through a second gate on to the minor road.

Follow the road steeply downhill keeping left, down the path from the mill drive entrance (a stream in wet weather), and soon enter Dorvel Wood (often muddy). Cross the stream and rise upon the principal path,

WALK 12
THE BARRINGTONS

The route goes along quiet paths and tracks to embrace Barrington Park and three enchanting Cotswold villages, as well as visiting three fine churches, two beautiful water mills and a lonely manor house.

ROUTE DIRECTIONS

Approx. 5¼ miles. Allow 2½ hours.
Park discreetly, close to the tree-shaded green in Windrush (grid ref. SP193131).
From the green beside St Peter's Church, advance west taking the lane right, which narrows as it descends, before rising to a flag stile. Cross the fence stile directly ahead, descending the bank to find a flag stile left and the path leading to Windrush Mill. Go right and left, round the millhouse①. From the stile follow the old meander of the river, right, to a gate, then angle left to another gate at mid-point along a fence, cross the ditch and meadow to a third gate over the newly dredged ditch, climbing through Friezeland Brake, proceeding uphill beside the hedge. Arriving at the gateway go left upon the track beside the hedge, keeping right round the Manor Farm buildings②. Continue north on the track which leads down between plantations and across open farmland to approach the site of Sherborne Mill.

Immediately after the young plantings at the foot of Mill Copse turn right uphill beside the wood, passing through the gap at the top, and angle across the field to the prominent peninsula of beeches. Follow the wooded strip and subsequent hedge. Turn right on to the bridle track in a south-easterly direction, eventually reaching the road across an old quarry. Turn right along the road.

Entering Great Barrington③, pass the war memorial to follow Mill Lane down to Barrington Mill. You may like to make a detour along the village street, switching back via Back Lane into Mill Lane, or follow the pavement right, down to the church④. Continue into Little Barrington via Strong's Causeway and the Fox Inn.

Beyond the mill cross the stile to traverse the meadow by a fenced path to a footbridge. You may go either way, but a left turn rising with the road and then veering right along Middle Road enables you to visit Little Barrington Church. Cross the top of the beautiful banked green, flanked by cottages and with a spring at its midst. Follow the footpath from Green Drive Farm crossing the fields via a series of stiles and gates, with Barrington Park to the right, to emerge at a kissing-gate on to the road in Windrush.

POINTS OF INTEREST

① Dating from the 17th century, Windrush Mill has a dignified charm, a scene embellished by doves and the constant gushings of the Windrush.

② Manor Farmhouse faces two contemporary barns; a late 17th-century composition designed to impress by their classical features.

③ An estate village firmly rooted in the best traditions of vernacular Cotswold architecture, with a working blacksmith's shop, though many of its houses are progressively undergoing much needed restoration work.

④ St Mary's is a large Norman church inevitably dominated by the monuments of the Bray and Talbot dynasties. Barrington Park, the great mansion adjoining it, was built for Earl Talbot in 1736–1738 by William Kent.

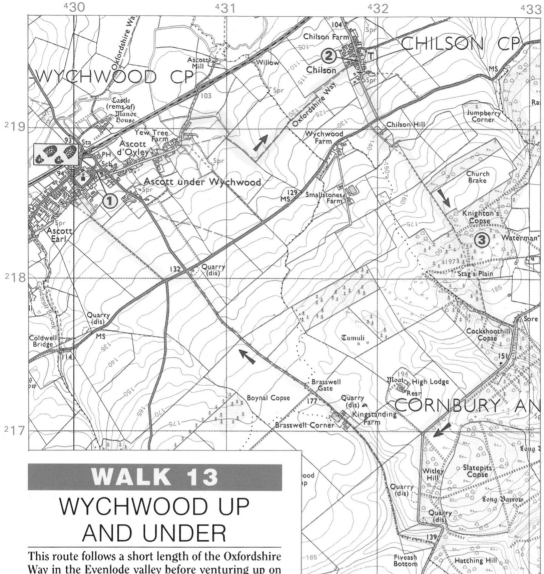

WALK 13
WYCHWOOD UP AND UNDER

This route follows a short length of the Oxfordshire Way in the Evenlode valley before venturing up on to Stag's Plain amid a remnant of the ancient Wychwood Forest. The walk features two delightful old forest communities and is a most pleasurable and unusual outing in a portion of the newly designated extension to the Cotswold Area of Outstanding Natural Beauty.

ROUTE DIRECTIONS

Approx. 6 miles. Allow 2½ hours.
Park near the green in Ascott-under-Wychwood (grid ref. SP302197).

From the old village school of Ascott-under-Wychwood①, follow High Street east through Ascott d'Oyley passing Willow Brook and Yew Tree Farm, on the lane leading to Ascott Mill. Diverge right (before the railway bridge) along the field margin directed by the Oxfordshire Way sign. Waymarks give sure guidance around field headlands and into Chilson②. Turn right up the street to the T-junction and go right and then first left, signed 'Chilson Hill only' ('circular walk' signs).

The path rises into Knighton's Copse③, cresting Stag's Plain. Zigzag left then right to descend the track between field and forest to double gates at Sore Leap. Go right on the minor road for one mile to Fiveash Bottom. Turn right along the track passing through Kingstanding Farm and once more over the ridge at Brasswell Gate, and down Brasswell Lane to the crossroads.

Turn left and then right, at the Leafield turn, down the track towards Ascott. Passing through a silage enclosure to a footpath sign, go through the gate, bear

right and immediately left; do not follow the track through Crown Farm. Follow the fence on the right down to the wall, go left 10yds to a stile and take the path between the gardens on to the street. Go right, then left along Church View, turning right to pass through the churchyard.

POINTS OF INTEREST

① The Ascott Martyrs are recorded on the seat surrounding the cherry tree on the green. It records the imprisonment of 16 village ladies in 1873 for the part they played in standing up for the rights of the humble agricultural worker.

② Chilson is a peaceful hamlet of thatch and Cotswold tiles, clustered along a short street, with barn conversions and a working farm. The name means that portion of an estate annexed and bequeathed to the youngest son of a nobleman.

③ Wychwood Forest, deriving its name from its location at the southern extremity of the lands of the Saxon Hwicce tribe, has been a deer chase and the private hunting ground of kings from those far off Saxon times. It has been jealously guarded throughout the centuries and public access is still strictly limited. The ancient custom of drawing water from Wortswell, variously known as 'Wassel' and 'Uzzel', deep in these Cornbury woods, is still practised by the villagers of Leafield and Finstock on Palm Sunday.

WALK 14

YES I REMEMBER ADLESTROP

Edward Thomas's short poem describing an unscheduled halt by the Oxford–Worcester train on 23 June 1914 continues to draw attention to this exquisite backwater. The oft-cited poem instils the eternal qualities held in a moment's observation, a private sensation many walkers will recognise. Thomas did not alight, nor ever know the charm of Adlestrop's rural environs, unlike Jane Austen, who visited the Rectory in 1806.

ROUTE DIRECTIONS

Approx. 4 miles. Allow 2 hours.
Start from Adlestrop Village Hall car park (grid ref. SP242272)

① From the footpath signboard, follow the green lane leading north. After the stile/gate, angle half-left across the ridge and furrow to a hunting gate in the corner of the field. Proceed to the gate on the left before the hovel, pass through, and keep ahead in the valley bottom to reach a gate.

Continue up the combe pasture, slanting slightly left up the slope to another gate and a short bank. Guided by marker posts cross the field to a metal gate on to the Conygree Lane track. Turn right shortly to enter the fringe of Peasewell Wood at a gate. At the top of the rise, and before the minor road, go right, through the hunting gate and along the open track atop Adlestrop Hill. Passing the viewfinder the track gently curves by a copse to a divergence of paths. Be guided down to the right by the yellow waymark arrow (with black spots). The path runs beside open farmland to enter Long Drive plantation, left, and emerges at a stile/gate on to the minor road; go right, ignoring the road to Fern Farm. Continue forward then turn left into the village of Adlestrop②.

Advance beyond the church and Adlestrop House③, following the lane via a kissing-gate down to a passage leading left, adjacent to the top lake. Pass through the cricket field enclosure via stiles and strike out south-west across the parkland to reach a stile on to the road. Go right, passing below the lake, to a stile on the right. Follow the streamside path to a footbridge, then cross the paddock to a hunting gate and keep foward across the drive and past the pond to join the road by Lower Farm stables.

POINTS OF INTEREST

① The bus shelter accommodates the last surviving GWR railway seat from the former Adlestrop station, immortalised by Edward Thomas in his poem which opens:

Yes, I remember Adlestrop
The name, because one afternoon
Of heat the express-train drew up there
Unwontedly. It was late June . . .

② Adlestrop Footpaths Committee is to be congratulated for its exemplary activities in opening up the beautiful rural surroundings to the village; be sure to purchase the guide (the excellent work of the Price family) which is available in the post office.

③ Theophilus Leigh, rector from 1718 to 1762 was Jane Austen's uncle. While she was staying with him, at what is now Adlestrop House, he learned that he had inherited Stoneleigh Hall, the modern home of the Royal Agricultural Society. She shared with him his first glimpse of that grand Warwickshire estate. Adlestrop House dates from the 17th century, and stands among magnificent cedar trees. The schoolroom, school house and a cottage close by are 19th century. The Church of St Mary Magdalene contains monuments to the Leigh family, who have owned Adlestrop Park since 1553.

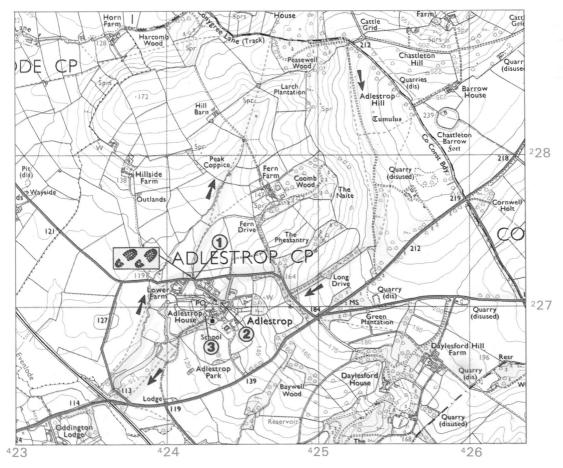

WALK 15
THE SLAUGHTERS

A fairly leisurely walk, much of it on firm ground, linking three of the most popular Cotswold villages.

ROUTE DIRECTIONS

Approx. 5¾ miles. Allow 2¼ hours.
Start from the large car park (small fee) in Bourton-on-the-Water (grid ref. SP171203).
Follow the path beside the river and cross the first footbridge left, keeping on the streamside path till the road bridge at the Motor Museum. Go right to the road junction and turn left. Turn right through the gateway, and head along the path passing the church①. Go left along Station Road and turn right along the path beside the Fosse Way (A429). Approaching the Coach and Horses, cross the main road to the gate on to the path across the fields; enter Lower Slaughter along the east bank of the River Eye②.

Keep beside the stream swinging round by Collett's Mill. Follow the Warden's Way sign along a passage to a kissing-gate behind the mill, proceeding beside the millpond to a second kissing-gate. Angle half-right to a stile traversing the ridge and furrow pasture to a handgate and descend to a further handgate and a tiny footbridge over the Eye, rising in a passage to the road. Go right crossing the road bridge, either to follow the road left or to pass through the gap beside the 'no through road' sign, then via the seat to a stile on to the causeway path leading to the stile next to the ford and stone footbridge③.

Ascend the road to enter the churchyard opposite the red telephone kiosk and reaching the church porch go left to enter the Square, then turn right. At the road junction go directly over to a gate climbing the bridle track. Bear right at the top through the gate following the green track to another gate, then pass by the farm cottages on to the road.

Go left following Buckle Street past Manor Farm and, after an old quarry on the right, bear right down the gated bridle track bound for Aston Mill. At the foot of the confined lane section, go left via a bridle gate, crossing the railway to a second bridle gate. The bridleway proceeds beside a fence and then open meadowland, via gates, on to the Fosse Way at Bourton Bridge④.

Follow Lansdown Road into Bourton, turning right at the sign opposite Mill Cottage. Cross a footbridge accompanying the footpath beside the River Windrush and passing through kissing-gates emerge into Sherborne Street. Turn left here and retrace your steps delightfully downstream.

POINTS OF INTEREST

① In 1784 the Norman church, on Saxon foundations, was demolished, and a Georgian church built on to the preserved chancel, thereby creating the only classical tower in the Cotswolds.

② The Manor Hotel is thought to be the work of Valentine Strong of Little Barrington about 1640. Dating from the 15th century the 'cottage-like' dovecote is the oldest building in the village, tucked behind the Manor and churchyard.

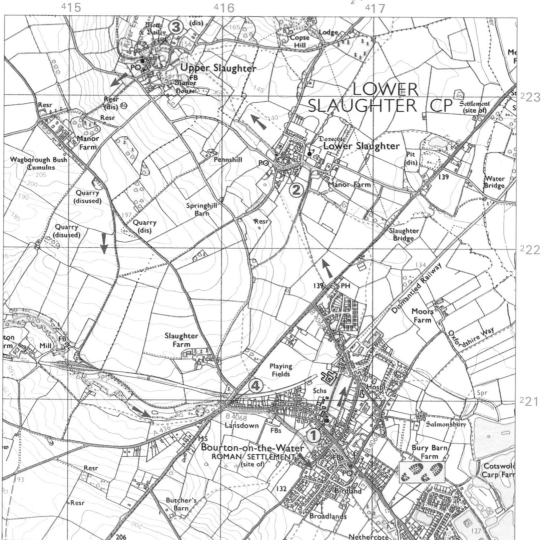

③ Upper Slaughter is a delightful village to peruse, particularly the streamside path. At the centre of the road circuit stands the mound of an early Norman castle, while the cottages abutting the churchyard were remodelled by Sir Edwin Lutyens.

④ A stone plaque on Bourton Bridge commemorates the Roman Second Legion, who built this section of the Fosse Way.

WALK 16
BOURTON DOWNS

Enjoy Cotswold countryside at its simplest on the uplands and in a seldom seen dry side-valley at the head of the River Dikler, tributary of the Windrush and, ultimately, the Thames. Vestigial sheepwalk pastures harbour herbs and insects, giving a special wildlife interest to the walk. At wet times several short muddy passages may be encountered along the route.

ROUTE DIRECTIONS

Approx. 5 miles. Allow 1¾ hours.
Park (SP133330) in lay-by between Smallthorns Cottages and Farm (where Ryknild Street crosses the unclassified road).
Follow the road south to Smallthorns Farm, turning left along the farm road to Bourton Far Hill Farm, maintain course via two gates and through the new deciduous plantation to a bridle gate.
  Go left, then right along the track beside the conifers, passing a tall, stone post. A few yards after switching right beside the fence take a left turn down a branch track to a gate, then bear left on the bank①. Contour through a shallow dip to a bridle gate entry into The Warren woodlands.
  The bridlepath passes through beautiful beechwoods, before becoming a track to descend the ridge to the minor road. Go right to the T-junction beside Hinchwick Manor② and turn right through the facing gate passing the sheep pen complex. Bear right of

Beechy Bank to follow the serpentine dry valley pasture north then west via gates ③, watchful for a critical switch right. The valley narrows and enters a hazel thicket passing the former loading bay of the old Hornleasow Quarry to join the unclassified road; turn right up hill to conclude the walk.

POINTS OF INTEREST

① The real charm of the walk lies in the opportunity it provides to study flora and fauna characteristic of ancient Cotswold grassland, in quiet seclusion from normal visitor haunts. The steep banks with their thin layer of soil support harebell, rockrose and thyme, intermingled with patches of gorse attracting a diversity of delicate butterflies particularly in July and August.

② Hinchwick Manor, dating from about 1830, was built around a courtyard. The original Old Hinchwick settlement survives a little to the south, closer to Condicote along Ryknild Street, as a cluster of fine old Cotswold barns.

③ At this point scrutinise the steep northern side of the valley to detect the zigzag shelf betraying the path of the Roman road, Ryknild Street. While the name stems from the pre-Roman British Iccenhilde, Ryknild Street has traditional Roman alignment, cutting straight across the grain of the countryside, linking the Fosse Way at Bourton-on-the-Water with a ford at Bradford-upon-Avon. The earliest roads developed from natural ridgeways, but the engineers of Ryknild Street were not deterred from their bee-line course by the folds in the wolds.

Page numbers in bold type indicate main entries.

ACKNOWLEDGEMENTS

The Automobile Association wishes to thank the following photographers, libraries
and associations for their assistance in the preparation of this book.

Corinium Museum 22/23 Pavement; *P W Dixon* 10 Long Barrow, 11 Crickley Hill, 24 Stoke Orchard,
24/25 Little Rissington; *S Dorey* 18/19 Nr Bibury; *Gloucester City Museum* 12 Birdlip; *Gloucester Shire
Hall* 9 Bisley, Cooper's Hill, 10 Hetty Pegler's Tump, 17 Farmland, 19 Ceramics, 20 Foss Way,
26 Cottages, 28 Cotswold Way, 28/29 Hiker, 30/31 Cam Long Down, 31 N Nibley, 32 Stanton; *Heart of
England Tourist Board* 8 Owlpen Manor, 32 Stanton Church; *Museum of English Rural Life* 44 Ewe,
58 Cotswolds Walls; *Nature Photographers Ltd* 13 Stonechat (T Andrewartha), Yellow Hammer
(C B Carver), 14 Tawny Owl (H Clark), Early Purple Orchid (D Bonsall), 15 Bird's-foot-trefoil, Peacock
Butterfly, Kingfisher (P R Sterry)

All remaining pictures are held in the Association's own library (AA Photo Library) with contributions
from: A Baker, A Lawson, S & O Mathews, R Rainford, A Souter, F Stephenson, R Surman, H Williams,
J Wyand

Other Ordnance Survey Maps of the Cotswolds

How to get there with Routemaster and Routeplanner Maps

Reach the Cotswolds from Birmingham, London, Cardiff and Southampton using Routemaster map sheets 7,
8 and 9. Alternatively use the Ordnance Survey Great Britain Routeplanner Map which covers the whole
country on one map sheet.

Exploring with Landranger and Tourist Maps

Landranger Series
1¼ inches to one mile or 1:50,000 scale.
These maps cover the whole of Britain and are
good for local motoring and walking. Each
contains tourist information such as parking,
picnic places, viewpoints and rights of way.
Sheets covering the Cotswolds are:

150 Worcester & the Malverns
151 Stratford-upon-Avon
163 Cheltenham & Cirencester
164 Oxford
172 Bristol & Bath
173 Swindon & Devizes

Tourist Map Series
1 inch to one mile or 1:63,360 scale
These maps cover popular holiday areas and are
ideal for discovering the countryside. In addition
to normal map detail ancient monuments,
camping and caravan sites, parking facilities and
viewpoints are marked. Lists of selected places of
interest are included on some sheets and others
include useful guides to the area.

Tourist Map Sheet 8 covers the Cotswolds

Other titles available in this series are:
Brecon Beacons; Channel Islands; Cornwall; Days
out from London; Devon and Exmoor; East
Anglia; Forest of Dean and Wye Valley; Ireland;
Isle of Wight; Lake District; New Forest;
Northumbria; North York Moors; Peak District;
Scottish Highlands; Snowdonia; South Downs;
Wessex; Yorkshire Dales